VERGIL
AENEID IX

Edited with
Introduction, Notes
& Vocabulary by

J. L. Whiteley

Published by Bristol Classical Press
General Editor: John H. Betts
(by arrangement with Macmillan & Co. Ltd.)

*Cover: Vergil from the Ara Pietatis Augustae
of Claudian date (41 - 54 A.D.), Villa Medici,
Rome*

Printed and bound in Great Britain
by Antony Rowe Ltd,
Chippenham, Wilts.

ISBN 0-906515-38-6

First published by Macmillan & Co. Ltd. (1955)

New edition (1979) published by Bristol Clas-
sical Press

Bristol Classical Press
Department of Classics
University of Bristol
Wills Memorial Building
Queens Road
BRISTOL   BS8 1RJ

CONTENTS

FOREWORD

THIS edition of Vergil's Aeneid, Book IX, has been prepared on the same principles as previous volumes in the Modern School Classics Series, and great care has been taken to write notes of a type best suited to the requirements of the school boy or girl of today, who is quite likely to embark on the preparation of the books set for the General Certificate of Education, Ordinary Level, without having previously read any continuous Latin texts at all.

The author wishes to thank Dr. Bertha Tilley for giving permission to use the illustrations on pp. 19, 27, 32, 39, from her book, *Vergil, Latium*.

J. L. W.

LONDON, 1954.

INTRODUCTION

PUBLIUS VERGILIUS MARO

VERGIL was born on October 15th, 70 B.C., at Andes
near Mantua in Cisalpine Gaul—the Lombardy plain.
Andes is usually identified with the present Pietole,
three miles from Mantua ; this identification, however,
has been rejected by some modern scholars, who favour
a site close to the existing towns of Carpendolo and
Calvisano.

The poet's family seems to have been of some local
importance, and his father, who owned and worked a
farm, was able to give his son the ancient equivalent
of a university education. Vergil studied at Cremona
and Milan, and later went to Rome to complete his
course in rhetoric and philosophy.

No doubt his father wished Vergil to make his way,
as Cicero had done, by his eloquence, first in the law
courts as a pleader, or barrister, and then in politics
by standing as a candidate for the various magistracies
which led ultimately to the consulship and a seat in
the senate. Vergil's temperament, however, for he
was shy, nervous, and awkward in society, was quite
unsuited to such a career, and after a single appearance
before a jury, he decided to devote his life to philosophy
and poetry.

Vergil returned to his native district, where he began

to write his first important work, the Eclogues, or Bucolics, ten poems, in semi-dramatic form, in which the persons are imaginary shepherds and their loves. This fashion of poetry, called ' pastoral ', was developed by the Sicilian Greek Theocritus. The Eclogues made Vergil's reputation as a poet and gained the attention of Maecenas, who at that time was the most trusted adviser in home affairs of Octavian, heir and successor of Julius Caesar, and destined shortly to become master of the Greco-Roman world as the first Roman Emperor, Augustus.

During this period of his life, in 41 B.C., Vergil was one of the many landed proprietors who saw their farms ruthlessly confiscated and allotted to demobilized soldiers—a common event during those troubled years of civil war which preceded the collapse of the Roman Republic. Fortunately for the poet, however, the fame of the Eclogues and his friendship with Maecenas made Vergil's position secure under the new régime, and enabled him to devote the rest of his life to poetical composition, free from all economic anxiety, at Naples and Nola in Campania.

Thus, in or about 37 B.C., Vergil began his second great work, the Georgics, a long poem, in four books, which describes the Roman methods of farming, the production of crops, of the vine and the olive, the breeding of stock and the keeping of bees. As we know from Vergil himself that he was asked to write on this subject by Maecenas, we may safely assume that his poem was designed as propaganda for Augustus' ' new order ' in Italy, and to reinforce that emperor's attempts to revive Roman religion, Roman agriculture, and the simple but hardy virtues which had made Rome great.

The two thousand odd lines of the poem were written very slowly, the years 37–30 B.C. being devoted to their composition, and reveal the highest standard of pure craftsmanship yet reached in Latin poetry. Moreover, though his subject in this poem might seem unlikely to produce great poetry, Vergil found the theme so congenial to his nature that he overcame the many difficulties, and not only produced a valuable text book for farmers, but also wrote some of the noblest poetry in the Latin language.

Soon after the completion of the Georgics, Vergil, now forty years of age, embarked, again no doubt at the instigation of his political patrons, upon his greatest and most ambitious work, the writing of an epic, i.e. a heroic narrative poem, the Aeneid, which should rival Homer's Iliad and Odyssey, and honour the imperial achievements of the Roman race, glorify the Roman character and focus Roman national sentiment on Augustus as the man sent by destiny to bring peace, stability and prosperity to the Greco-Roman world, which had been racked for so many years by civil war, fear and uncertainty.

The Aeneid occupied Vergil's whole attention for the remaining years of his life. In 19 B.C., after a

journey to the East, he fell ill on his return to Italy
at Brundisium. His health had never been robust,
and realizing that his end was near, he gave instructions
that the great epic, for which he had planned a three
years' revision, and of whose imperfections, as an
intensely self-critical artist, he was very conscious,
should be destroyed. This instruction, fortunately
for literature, was disregarded by the poet's literary
executors.

The Aeneid is an epic poem in twelve books, and tells
how a Trojan prince, Aeneas, a survivor from the sack
of Troy by the Greeks, is directed by the gods to seek
a new home in Italy. In that land, after many
vicissitudes, he settles with his Trojan companions,
colonists from whom the Romans liked to believe that
they were sprung. Into this legend Vergil weaves a
glorification of the family of Augustus, connecting the
Julian clan, to which it belonged, with Iulus, the son
of Aeneas.

Criticism of the poem has always recognized its
superlative artistry, despite Vergil's own dissatis-
faction with its lack of final polish, and is unanimous
in detecting in Vergil's mind and reflected by the
poem, a profound sensibility and sympathy with
human troubles, which are hardly paralleled in Latin
literature. In so far as judgment has been adverse,
it has fastened on the character of the hero, Aeneas
himself, in whom the virtue of *pietas*, ' dutifulness ',
whether towards father, country or gods, is allowed

prominence at the expense of warmer and more human feelings.

The story of the epic, book by book, is as follows :

BOOK I.   Aeneas and his companions are driven by a storm aroused by Juno, implacable enemy of the Trojan race, towards the North African coast, where, thanks to tne intervention of Neptune, most of the ships find shelter, their crews landing safely and making their way to Carthage. In this city, which has just been founded by Dido, a young widowed princess from Tyre, they are hospitably received by the queen, who, at a banquet, invites Aeneas to relate the story of his wanderings.

BOOK II.   The Trojan hero begins his narrative with the story of the final siege, capture and sack of Troy. We hear of the treacherous Sinon, who feigned to be a deserter persecuted by his Greek fellows in order to gain entrance to the city, of the trick of the Wooden Horse, the cruel death of Laocoon and his sons, who sought to warn the Trojans of their approaching doom, the entry of the Greeks, their murder of King Priam, and the escape of Aeneas from the burning city with his aged father Anchises, his young son Iulus, known also as Ascanius, and the household gods. In the confusion his wife Creusa is lost, but later Aeneas meets her ghost and is told that he is destined to found a new kingdom in Italy.

BOOK III.   The narrative continues with the escape of Aeneas and his Trojan comrades from the mainland,

and their voyage to various places in search of the
' promised land '—to Thrace, Delos, Crete, and finally
to the West, by way of the Strophades Islands, and
the coast of Epirus (Albania), where Aeneas is advised
by Helenus to sail round Sicily, to make for the west
coast of Italy, and there to consult a prophetess, the
Sibyl, at Cumae, and to appease Juno. Aeneas does
as Helenus suggests, and thus, after seven years'
wandering over the Eastern Mediterranean, he arrives
at the western end of Sicily, where he spends the winter.
Aeneas concludes his narrative to the queen, his hostess,
by recording the death in Sicily of his father, Anchises.

BOOK IV. Meanwhile Dido, who has been greatly
attracted to Aeneas from the first owing to the influence
of Venus, his mother, now falls more and more deeply
in love with him. Shortly after his arrival at Carthage,
Dido and Aeneas by the power of Juno and Venus, who
from quite different motives favour such a development,
become lovers. Jupiter, however, now intervenes, and
warns Aeneas, through Mercury, that he must leave
Africa at once and fulfil his destined task of founding a
new realm in Italy. Realizing the strength of Dido's
passion for him, he tries to depart secretly, but his inten-
tions become known to her. Yet he remains unmoved
by her entreaties, which turn in the end to words of
scorn and hatred. As he sails away, Dido destroys
herself.

BOOK V. Aeneas returns to western Sicily and there
celebrates the anniversary of his father's death with

funeral games.[1] During the latter, Juno persuades the
Trojan women, weary as they are of their wanderings,
to set fire to the ships, but a sudden rain-storm subdues
the flames and only four are destroyed. The Trojans
sail away from Sicily. On the voyage Palinurus, the
helmsman, is overcome by sleep, and falling overboard,
is drowned.

BOOK VI. In this, to many readers the finest book
of the poem, Aeneas, having at last set foot on the
coast of Western Italy, visits the Sibyl of Cumae and
receives from her directions for the visit he longs to
pay to the underworld. Armed with the ' golden
bough ', which alone can procure him access to the
nether regions of Hades, he traverses the various
quarters of that kingdom, and meets the spirit of his
father, who parades for Aeneas the souls of all great
Romans that are awaiting incarnation.[2] In this way
Vergil is able to give his readers a kind of national
cavalcade of all the great figures in Roman history
from the earliest times down to his own day. Thus the
pageant closes with the greatest figure of them all, the
emperor Augustus.

The sixth book contains the famous lines (851–3),

---

[1] The elaborate account of these games, which occupies most of
Book V, is no doubt due to the influence of Homer, who in the *Iliad*
describes at great length the funeral games of the hero Patroclus.

[2] Note again Vergil's indebtedness to Homer. Odysseus, too, in
Book XI of the *Odyssey*, is made to visit the underworld.

which epitomize the Roman's pride in the city's greatness as an imperial power :

> Tu regere imperio populos, Romane, memento ;
> Hae tibi erunt artes ; pacisque imponere morem,
> Parcere subiectis, et debellare superbos.

> ' Thou, O Roman, remember to rule the nations 'neath thy sway,
> These shall be thine arts, to impose the laws of peace,
> To spare the conquered and to chasten the proud in war.'

BOOK VII. Aeneas at last enters his promised land by the mouth of the river Tiber, the natural frontier between the districts of Latium, lying south of the river, and Etruria to the north. He is welcomed by Latinus, king of Latium, who sees in Aeneas the bridegroom for his daughter Lavinia, for whom he has been advised by an oracle to find a foreign husband.

Turnus, however, chieftain of the neighbouring Rutuli, and worthiest of Lavinia's suitors, is enraged at the proposal of Latinus, and, supported by Amata the latter's queen, arouses the Latins against the Trojans. The book closes with a magnificent catalogue of the Italian forces—another epic convention, originating in Homer's catalogue of the Greek ships in the *Iliad*, Book II.

BOOK VIII. The river god Tiberinus sends Aeneas to seek aid from a Greek, Evander, who has settled on the Palatine Hill in what is destined to be the future Rome. Evander promises help and conducts Aeneas through the city, explaining the origin of various Roman sites and names. Venus persuades Vulcan, her husband, to make Aeneas a suit of armour and a shield,[1] on which are depicted in relief various events in the future history of Rome, down to the battle of Actium, 31 B.C., by which Vergil's patron Augustus gained undisputed sovereignty over the ancient world.

BOOK IX. While Aeneas is absent, Turnus makes an attempt, barely frustrated, to storm the Trojan camp by the Tiber, and is successful in setting fire to their ships. Nisus and Euryalus, two Trojans, endeavour to slip through the enemy lines in order to inform Aeneas of the critical situation. They slay some of the foe, but are eventually discovered and killed. The next day, when Turnus renews his assault, he succeeds in entering the camp, but is cut off, and only effects his escape by plunging into the Tiber.

BOOK X. A council of the gods is held in Olympus and Jupiter decides to leave the issue of the war to fate. Aeneas now wins the support of an Etruscan army which has revolted against the cruelties of the king, Mezentius, and joined by reinforcements from Evander under the leadership of the latter's son, Pallas, he returns to aid the hard-pressed Trojans. In the furious fighting Mezentius and his son Lausus are slain, but Turnus kills Pallas.

---

[1] Homer, too, in the *Iliad* Book XVIII, describes at length a shield, that of the Greek hero, Achilles.

Book XI. A truce is arranged for the burial of the dead. On the arrival of an embassy from the Latins, Aeneas offers to settle the issue with a single combat between himself and Turnus. The Latins hold a council of war and determine to continue the struggle, but they are defeated a second time by the Trojans and their allies in spite of many deeds of valour, especially on the part of Camilla, a warrior maiden who is killed in the fighting.

Book XII. Another truce is arranged, and Turnus agrees to accept Aeneas' challenge, despite the opposition of the queen Amata and his sister, Juturna. The latter provokes the Latins to violate the truce. In the ensuing struggle Aeneas is wounded, but is miraculously healed by his mother, the goddess Venus. He returns to the fray, routs the Latins and Rutulians and eventually meets Turnus in single combat. The Rutulian chieftain is wounded and rendered helpless. Aeneas is minded to spare him until he notices that he is wearing the belt of the dead Pallas, whereupon he slays him.

The Metre of the Poem

Most English verse consists of lines in which stressed syllables alternate with unstressed, as for example in the lines :

'The ploughman homeward plods his weary way,

And leaves the world to darkness and to me.'

Such verse is called *accentual*.

The principle of Greek and Latin verse is different. It is based on the rhythmical arrangement of long and short syllables, the long syllables taking twice as long to pronounce as the short. This system may be compared with music, long syllables corresponding to *crotchets* and short to *quavers*, one *crotchet* being equal to two *quavers*. This type of verse is called *quantitative*.

Just as, to appreciate the rhythm of English verse, you are taught to *scan*, i.e. to divide the lines into *feet* and mark the stress in each foot, so you must learn to scan Latin verse by a similar division into feet by marking the syllables long (–) or short (⌣). Not only is it necessary to do this in order to understand the construction of the verse and the musical qualities of the poetry, but the ability to do so is a great help in translation, by making it possible to distinguish words alike in spelling but different in *quantity*, for example, *pŏpŭlŭs*, ' people ', from *pōpŭlŭs*, ' poplar tree ', and *mīsĕrĕ*, ' they sent ', from *mĭsĕrē*, ' pitifully '.

The verses of the Aeneid are called heroic hexameters. In this verse two kinds of feet, or bars, are found. One is the *dactyl*, a long syllable followed by two short syllables, the other, the *spondee*, two long syllables. Each line, or hexameter, contains six feet, the first four of which may be either dactyls or spondees, the fifth being almost always a dactyl and the sixth a spondee. In place of this sixth-foot spondee a trochee (_ ◡) is allowable.

Thus the scheme of the hexameter is as follows :

I	2	3	4	5	6
_ ◡ ◡	_ ◡ ◡	_ ◡ ◡	_ ◡ ◡	_ ◡ ◡	_ _
or _ _	_ _	_ _	_ _		_ ◡

In the scansion of these lines, no account is taken of syllables at the close of words *ending* in a vowel or an *m*, if they are followed immediately by a word *commencing* with a vowel or an *h*. Such a final syllable is said to be *elided*, ' struck out ', though it was more probably slurred in pronunciation. Thus in l. 3 of the present book,

audacem ad Turnum. luco tum forte parentis

the final *em* of *audacem* is ignored in scanning.

A long syllable is one that contains a vowel long *by*

nature, or a diphthong ; or a vowel, naturally short that is long *by position*, i.e. is followed by two consonants.

A short syllable is one that contains a vowel short *by nature* and ends either with no consonant, or with only one.

The two consonants which have been mentioned as having the effect of lengthening a syllable need not both occur in the same word. Thus in l. 2 *-it* is long, though the *i* is naturally short, because that *i* is followed by a *t* and the *s* of *Saturnia*.

PROSODY

The following information about the *quantity* of Latin syllables will be found useful.

A. Relating to all syllables.

All diphthongs are long, except before another vowel.

B. Relating to final syllables.

1. Final *a* is usually short.
Except
   (*a*) in the abl. sg. of 1st decl. nouns, e.g. *mensā* ;
   (*b*) in the 2nd sg. imperative active of 1st conjugation verbs, e.g. *amā* ;
   (*c*) in indeclinable words such as *intereā, frustrā*.

2. Final *e* is usually short.
Except
   (*a*) in the abl. sg. of 5th decl. nouns, e.g. *aciē* ;
   (*b*) in the 2nd sg. imperative active of 2nd conjugation verbs, e.g. *monē* ;

    (*c*) in adverbs formed from adjectives of the 1st and 2nd declensions, e.g. *pulchrē*, from *pulcher*, *-chra*, *-chrum*. (Note, however, *benĕ*, *malĕ*.)

3. Final *i* is usually long.

Except in *mihi*, *tibi*, *sibi*, *ubi*, *ibi*, in which it may be long or short, and in *quasi*, *nisi*.

4. Final *o* is usually long.

Except in *modo*, *duo*, *ego*.

5. Final *u* is always long.

C. Final syllables of words of more than one syllable, ending in any single consonant other than *s*, are short.

Except

    (*a*) *dispār* ;

    (*b*) in the perfects *iīt* and *petiīt*.

D. 1. Final *as*, *os*, *es*, are long.

Except

    (*a*) *compŏs*, *penĕs* ;

    (*b*) in nominatives singular in *es* of 3rd declension nouns (consonant stems) having genitive singular in *-ĕtis*, *-ĭtis,-ĭdis* ; e.g. *segĕs*, *milĕs*, *obsĕs*. (But note *pariēs*, *abiēs*.)

    (*c*) In compounds of *es* (from *sum*), e.g. *abĕs*, *prodĕs*.

2. Final *us* and *is* are short.

Except *ūs*

    (*a*) in gen. sg., nom., voc. and acc. pl. of 4th decl. nouns, e.g. *gradūs* ;

(*b*) in the nom. sg. of consonant stem 3rd decl.
nouns having gen. sg. with a long syllable
before the last, e.g. *tellūs* (*-ūris*), *palūs* (*-ūdis*),
virtūs (*-ūtis*).

And except *īs*

(*c*) in dat. and abl. pl., e.g., *mensīs, dominīs, vinīs* ;
(*d*) in acc. pl. of 3rd decl. *-i* stems, e.g. *navīs,
omnīs* ;
(*e*) in the 2nd pers. sg. of 4th conjugation verbs,
e.g. *audīs* ; and in *sīs*, and compounds of *sīs*,
as *possīs* ; and in *velīs, nolīs, malīs*, and *īs*
(from *eo*).

E. Quantity of syllables determined by position in the
same word.

1. A syllable ending with a vowel or diphthong,
immediately followed by a syllable beginning with a
vowel, or with *h* and a vowel, is short ; e.g. *vĭa, prăe-
ustus, trăhit.*

Except

(*a*) in the case of genitives in *ius*, e.g. *alīus, solīus,
utrīus.* (But note *illĭus.*)
(*b*) *e* preceding *i* in 5th decl. nouns, e.g. *diĕi*, and
ĕi (from *is*).
(*c*) the syllable *fĭ* in *fĭo.* (But note *fĭeri, fĭerem*,
the *i* being short before *er.*)

2. A syllable containing a vowel immediately fol-
lowed by two consonants, or by *x* or *z*, which are really
double consonants (*cs* and *ds*) is long ; e.g. the second
syllable in *regent, auspex.*

Except if the two consonants are a combination of one of the following, *b, c, d, f, g, p, t*, with (following) *l* or *r*. If a short vowel precedes such a combination, the syllable is not necessarily long.

Finally, it must be remembered that these rules apply to Latin words only, and not to many Greek proper names which will be encountered in this book.

Let us see now if, with the information given above, we can scan one of the hexameters of this book. Looking at line 3 for example,

audacem ad Turnum. luco tum forte parentis

(i) in this the final *em* of *audacem* will be disregarded before the initial vowel of *ad*.

(ii) Mark long (–) all syllables whose long quantity can be determined by the rules given above.

ad, tur, num, tum, for, en

are all long syllables (by Rule E 2).

So is *co* by Rule B 4.

(iii) Mark short (⌣) all syllables whose short quantity can be determined by rule. The *e* of *forte* is short (by Rule B 2), and the *is* of *parentis* by Rule D 2.

Thus we now have:

audācem ad Tūrnūm. lūcō tūm fortĕ parentĭs

Generally speaking, it will be found that such an application of the rules of prosody will give enough syllables of known quantity to make it possible to scan the line completely.

To do this, work backwards from the end of the line because the pattern of the last two feet

$$(- \smile \smile \mid - - \text{ or } - \smile)$$

is constant.

This gives us for these feet :

$$\textit{fort}\bar{e}\ \textit{p\breve{a}rent\breve{i}s}$$

Working backwards again we shall find that the fourth, third, second and first feet are spondees.

Thus the whole line, divided into feet and with the quantities marked is :

$$\bar{a}ud\bar{a} \mid \overline{cem\ ad}\ T\bar{u}r \mid n\breve{u}m.\ l\bar{u} \mid c\bar{o}\ \ t\breve{u}m \mid fort\breve{e}\ p\breve{a} \mid rent\breve{i}s$$

One thing remains to be done before the scansion is complete. It is a rule that, usually in the third foot, more rarely in the fourth, one word must end and another begin. This is called the *caesura* or ' cutting '. If the break occurs after the first syllable of the foot, the caesura is said to be strong ; if after the second, weak. In this line we obviously have a strong caesura in the third foot. The caesura is regularly marked in scansion by a pair of vertical lines. Thus the scansion of the line, as completed, is

$$\bar{a}ud\bar{a} \mid \overline{cem\ ad}\ T\bar{u}r \mid n\breve{u}m. \parallel l\bar{u} \mid c\bar{o}\ \ t\breve{u}m \mid fort\breve{e}\ p\breve{a} \mid rent\breve{i}s$$

You will find that with careful attention to the pronunciation of Latin words, you will gradually learn to scan by ear, without the necessity of applying for help to the rules of prosody.

Note that the scheme of the hexameter makes it elastic, and gives it variable length, as long as 17 or as short as 13 syllables. This makes possible such onomatopoeic lines as .

$$\bar{Qua}dr\breve{u}p\breve{e}\text{-} \mid \bar{da}n\breve{te}\; p\breve{u}\text{-} \mid tr\bar{em} \parallel \bar{so}n\breve{i}\text{-} \mid t\bar{u}\; qu\breve{a}t\breve{i}t \mid \bar{u}ng\breve{u}l\breve{a} \mid$$

$$\bar{ca}mp\breve{u}m$$

(where the poet, describing the galloping of horses, imitates the sound of them) ; and as

$$\bar{ill}(i)\; \bar{i}n\text{-} \mid t\bar{e}r\; s\bar{e}\text{-} \mid s\bar{e} \parallel m\bar{u}l\text{-} \mid t\bar{a}\; v\bar{i} \mid br\bar{a}cch\breve{i}\breve{a} \mid t\bar{o}ll\bar{u}nt$$

(where again sound is matched to sense, for the line describes the alternate blows upon an anvil delivered by two smiths).

VERGIL

AENEID IX

*Juno sends Iris to Turnus to urge him to make a surprise attack
on the Trojan camp in the absence of Aeneas.*

Atque ea diversa penitus dum parte geruntur,
Irim de caelo misit Saturnia Iuno
audacem ad Turnum. luco tum forte parentis
Pilumni Turnus sacrata valle sedebat.
ad quem sic roseo Thaumantias ore locuta est :   5
' Turne, quod optanti divum promittere nemo
auderet, volvenda dies en attulit ultro.
Aeneas urbe et sociis et classe relicta
sceptra Palatini sedemque petit Euandri.
nec satis : extremas Corythi penetravit ad urbes   10
Lydorumque manum, collectos armat agrestes.
quid dubitas? nunc tempus equos, nunc poscere currus.
rumpe moras omnes et turbata arripe castra.'
dixit, et in caelum paribus se sustulit alis
ingentemque fuga secuit sub nubibus arcum.   15
agnovit iuvenis duplicesque ad sidera palmas
sustulit, ac tali fugientem est voce secutus :
' Iri, decus caeli, quis te mihi nubibus actam
detulit in terras? unde haec tam clara repente
tempestas? medium video discedere caelum   20
palantesque polo stellas. sequor omina tanta,
quisquis in arma vocas.' et sic effatus ad undam

processit summoque hausit de gurgite lymphas,
multa deos orans, oneravitque aethera votis.

*The attack is launched and the Trojans, following the orders of
Aeneas, retire within their camp.*

iamque omnis campis exercitus ibat apertis,　　25
dives equum, dives pictaï vestis et auri—
Messapus primas acies, postrema coercent
Tyrrhidae iuvenes, medio dux agmine Turnus—,
[vertitur arma tenens et toto vertice supra est].
ceu septem surgens sedatis amnibus altus　　30
per tacitum Ganges aut pingui flumine Nilus
cum refluit campis et iam se condidit alveo.
hic subitam nigro glomerari pulvere nubem
prospiciunt Teucri ac tenebras insurgere campis.
primus ab adversa conclamat mole Caïcus :　　35
' quis globus, o cives, caligine volvitur atra?
ferte citi ferrum, date tela, ascendite muros,
hostis adest, heia! ' ingenti clamore per omnes
condunt se Teucri portas et moenia complent.
namque ita discedens praeceperat optimus armis　　40
Aeneas : si qua interea fortuna fuisset,
neu struere auderent aciem neu credere campo ;
castra modo et tutos servarent aggere muros.
ergo etsi conferre manum pudor iraque monstrat,
obiciunt portas tamen et praecepta facessunt,　　45
armatique cavis exspectant turribus hostem.

Turnus' challenge to the Trojans meets no response.   Thereupon he
incites his men to set fire to the Trojan fleet beached near by.

Turnus, ut ante volans tardum praecesserat agmen
viginti lectis equitum comitatus et urbi
improvisus adest (maculis quem Thracius albis
portat equus cristaque tegit galea aurea rubra),   50
' ecquis erit, mecum, iuvenes, qui primus in hostem—?
en,' ait et iaculum attorquens emittit in auras,
principium pugnae, et campo sese arduus infert.
clamorem excipiunt socii fremituque sequuntur
horrisono, Teucrum mirantur inertia corda,   55
non aequo dare se campo, non obvia ferre
arma viros, sed castra fovere. huc turbidus atque huc
lustrat equo muros aditumque per avia quaerit.
ac veluti pleno lupus insidiatus ovili
cum fremit ad caulas, ventos perpessus et imbres   60
nocte super media ; tuti sub matribus agni
balatum exercent, ille asper et improbus ira
saevit in absentes, collecta fatigat edendi
ex longo rabies et siccae sanguine fauces :
haud aliter Rutulo muros et castra tuenti   65
ignescunt irae ; duris dolor ossibus ardet.
qua temptet ratione aditus, et quae via clausos
excutiat Teucros vallo atque effundat in aequor?
classem, quae lateri castrorum adiuncta latebat,
aggeribus saeptam circum et fluvialibus undis,   70
invadit, sociosque incendia poscit ovantes
atque manum pinu flagranti fervidus implet.
tum vero incumbunt (urget praesentia Turni),

atque omnis facibus pubes accingitur atris.
diripuere focos ; piceum fert fumida lumen   75
taeda et commixtam Volcanus ad astra favillam.

Now Cybele, the mother-goddess, had prayed to Jupiter that the
   timbers from the sacred grove which she gave to Aeneas for his
   ships be safe from storm and blast. Unable to grant her
   prayer in full, Jupiter had promised that on arrival in Italy
   the ships would become sea-goddesses.

quis deus, o Musae, tam saeva incendia Teucris
avertit? tantos ratibus quis depulit ignes? ·
dicite. prisca fides facto, sed fama perennis.
tempore quo primum Phrygia formabat in Ida   80
Aeneas classem et pelagi petere alta parabat,
ipsa deum fertur genetrix Berecyntia magnum
vocibus his adfata Iovem : ' da, nate, petenti,
quod tua cara parens domito te poscit Olympo.
[pinea silva mihi, multos dilecta per annos,]   85
lucus in arce fuit summa, quo sacra ferebant,
nigranti picea trabibusque obscurus acernis :
has ego Dardanio iuveni, cum classis egeret,
laeta dedi ; nunc sollicitam timor anxius angit.
solve metus atque hoc precibus sine posse parentem,
ne cursu quassatae ullo neu turbine venti   91
vincantur ; prosit nostris in montibus ortas.'
filius huic contra, torquet qui sidera mundi :
' o genetrix, quo fata vocas? aut quid petis istis?
mortaline manu factae immortale carinae   95
fas habeant? certusque incerta pericula lustret
Aeneas? cui tanta deo permissa potestas?

immo, ubi defunctae finem portusque tenebunt
Ausonios olim, quaecumque evaserit undis
Dardaniumque ducem Laurentia vexerit arva, 100
mortalem eripiam formam, magnique iubebo
aequoris esse deas, qualis Nereïa Doto
et Galatea secant spumantem pectore pontum.'
dixerat, idque ratum Stygii per flumina fratris,
per pice torrentes atraque voragine ripas 105
adnuit et totum nutu tremefecit Olympum.

The promise is fulfilled.

ergo aderat promissa dies et tempora Parcae
debita complerant, cum Turni iniuria Matrem
admonuit ratibus sacris depellere taedas.
hic primum nova lux oculis offulsit et ingens 110
visus ab Aurora caelum transcurrere nimbus
Idaeique chori ; tum vox horrenda per auras
excidit et Troum Rutulorumque agmina complet :
' ne trepidate meas, Teucri, defendere naves,
neve armate manus ; maria ante exurere Turno 115
quam sacras dabitur pinus. vos ite solutae,
ite deae pelagi ; genetrix iubet.' et sua quaeque
continuo puppes abrumpunt vincula ripis
delphinumque modo demersis aequora rostris
ima petunt. hinc virgineae (mirabile monstrum)
[quot prius aeratae steterant ad litora prorae] 121
reddunt se totidem facies pontoque feruntur.

*Turnus rallies his followers, dismayed at the portent, with a
stirring speech and the Trojan camp is closely beset.*

   obstipuere animis Rutuli, conterritus ipse
turbatis Messapus equis, cunctatur et amnis
rauca sonans revocatque pedem Tiberinus ab alto.
at non audaci Turno fiducia cessit ;   126
ultro animos tollit dictis atque increpat ultro :
' Troianos haec monstra petunt, his Iuppiter ipse
auxilium solitum eripuit ; non tela neque ignes
exspectant Rutulos. ergo maria invia Teucris,   130
nec spes ulla fugae ; rerum pars altera adempta est,
terra autem in nostris manibus, tot milia gentes
arma ferunt Italae. nil me Italia terrent,
si qua Phryges prae se iactant, responsa deorum :
sat fatis Venerique datum, tetigere quod arva   135
fertilis Ausoniae Troës. sunt et mea contra
fata mihi, ferro sceleratam exscindere gentem,
coniuge praerepta ; nec solos tangit Atridas
iste dolor, solisque licet capere arma Mycenis.
" sed periisse semel satis est " : peccare fuisset   140
ante satis, penitus modo non genus omne perosos
femineum. quibus haec medii fiducia valli
fossarumque morae, leti discrimina parva,
dant animos. at non viderunt moenia Troiae
Neptuni fabricata manu considere in ignes?   145
sed vos, o lecti, ferro quis scindere vallum
apparat et mecum invadit trepidantia castra?
non armis mihi Volcani, non mille carinis
est opus in Teucros. addant se protinus omnes

Etrusci socios. tenebras et inertia furta   150
[Palladii, caesis summae custodibus arcis]
ne timeant, nec equi caeca condemur in alvo ;
luce palam certum est igni circumdare muros.
haud sibi cum Danais rem faxo et pube Pelasga
esse ferant, decimum quos distulit Hector in annum.
nunc adeo, melior quoniam pars acta diei,   156
quod superest, laeti bene gestis corpora rebus
procurate, viri, et pugnam sperate parari.'
interea vigilum excubiis obsidere portas
cura datur Messapo et moenia cingere flammis.   160
bis septem Rutuli, muros qui milite servent
delecti, ast illos centeni quemque sequuntur
purpurei cristis iuvenes auroque corusci.
discurrunt variantque vices, fusique per herbam
indulgent vino et vertunt crateras aënos.   165
conlucent ignes, noctem custodia ducit
insomnem ludo.
     haec super e vallo prospectant Troës et armis
alta tenent, nec non trepidi formidine portas
explorant, pontesque et propugnacula iungunt,   170
tela gerunt. instat Mnestheus acerque Serestus,
quos pater Aeneas, si quando adversa vocarent,
rectores iuvenum et rerum dedit esse magistros.
omnis per muros legio sortita periclum
excubat exercetque vices, quod cuique tuendum est.

Nisus and his youthful companion Euryalus are introduced. The former proposes to make his way stealthily to Aeneas to bring him back to aid the beleaguered camp. Euryalus refuses the chance not to accompany him.

Nisus erat portae custos, acerrimus armis,   176
Hyrtacides, comitem Aeneae quem miserat Ida
venatrix iaculo celerem levibusque sagittis ;
et iuxta comes Euryalus, quo pulchrior alter
non fuit Aeneadum Troiana neque induit arma,   180
ora puer prima signans intonsa iuventa.
his amor unus erat pariterque in bella ruebant ;
tum quoque communi portam statione tenebant.
Nisus ait : ' dine hunc ardorem mentibus addunt,
Euryale, an sua cuique deus fit dira cupido?   185
aut pugnam aut aliquid iamdudum invadere magnum
mens agitat mihi, nec placida contenta quiete est.
cernis quae Rutulos habeat fiducia rerum.
lumina rara micant, somno vinoque soluti
procubuere, silent late loca.   percipe porro   190
quid dubitem et quae nunc animo sententia surgat.
Aenean acciri omnes, populusque patresque,
exposcunt, mittique viros qui certa reportent.
si tibi quae posco promittunt (nam mihi facti
fama sat est), tumulo videor reperire sub illo   195
posse viam ad muros et moenia Pallantea.'
obstipuit magno laudum percussus amore
Euryalus, simul his ardentem adfatur amicum :
'mene igitur socium summis adiungere rebus,
Nise, fugis? solum te in tanta pericula mittam?   200
non ita me genitor, bellis adsuetus Opheltes,

Argolicum terrorem inter Troiaeque labores
sublatum erudiit, nec tecum talia gessi
magnanimum Aenean et fata extrema secutus :
est hic, est animus lucis contemptor et istum   205
qui vita bene credat emi, quo tendis, honorem.'
Nisus ad haec : 'equidem de te nil tale verebar,
nec fas, non : ita me referat tibi magnus ovantem
Iuppiter aut quicumque oculis haec aspicit aequis.
sed si quis (quae multa vides discrimine tali)   210
si quis in adversum rapiat casusve deusve,
te superesse velim ; tua vita dignior aetas.
sit qui me raptum pugna pretiove redemptum
mandet humo, solita aut si qua id Fortuna vetabit,
absenti ferat inferias decoretque sepulchro.   215
neu matri miserae tanti sim causa doloris,
quae te sola, puer, multis e matribus ausa
persequitur, magni nec moenia curat Acestae.'
ille autem ' causas nequiquam nectis inanes,
nec mea iam mutata loco sententia cedit.   220
acceleremus ' ait, vigiles simul excitat. illi
succedunt servantque vices : statione relicta
ipse comes Niso graditur regemque requirunt.

Nisus seeks audience of the Trojan chiefs and outlines his plan
which wins enthusiastic support and promise of great rewards
from Ascanius, Aeneas' son. Euryalus moves his audience
by his appeal for his aged mother. Ascanius promises all he
asks and the two heroes are escorted to the gate.

cetera per terras omnes animalia somno
laxabant curas et corda oblita laborum ;   225
ductores Teucrum primi, delecta iuventus,
consilium summis regni de rebus habebant,
quid facerent quisve Aeneae iam nuntius esset.
stant longis adnixi hastis et scuta tenentes
castrorum et campi medio. tum Nisus et una   230
Euryalus confestim alacres admittier orant,
rem magnam pretiumque morae fore. primus Iulus
accepit trepidos ac Nisum dicere iussit.
tum sic Hyrtacides : ' audite o mentibus aequis,
Aeneadae, neve haec nostris spectentur ab annis,   235
quae ferimus. Rutuli somno vinoque soluti
conticuere; locum insidiis conspeximus ipsi,
qui patet in bivio portae quae proxima ponto ;
interrupti ignes, aterque ad sidera fumus
erigitur ; si fortuna permittitis uti,   240
quaesitum Aenean et moenia Pallantea,
mox hic cum spoliis ingenti caede peracta
adfore cernetis. nec nos via fallit euntes :
vidimus obscuris primam sub vallibus urbem
venatu adsiduo et totum cognovimus amnem.'   245
hic annis gravis atque animi maturus Aletes :
' di patrii, quorum semper sub numine Troia est,
non tamen omnino Teucros delere paratis,

cum tales animos iuvenum et tam certa tulistis
pectora.'—sic memorans umeros dextrasque tenebat
amborum et vultum lacrimis atque ora rigabat—   251
' quae vobis, quae digna, viri, pro laudibus istis
praemia posse rear solvi? pulcherrima primum
di moresque dabunt vestri ; tum cetera reddet
actutum pius Aeneas atque integer aevi   255
Ascanius, meriti tanti non immemor umquam.'
' immo ego vos, cui sola salus genitore reducto,'
excipit Ascanius, ' per magnos, Nise, penates
Assaracique larem et canae penetralia Vestae
obtestor, quaecumque mihi fortuna fidesque est,   260
in vestris pono gremiis ; revocate parentem,
reddite conspectum ; nihil illo triste recepto.   ⁊ abl. absolute
bina dabo argento perfecta atque aspera signis
pocula, devicta genitor quae cepit Arisba,   ⁊ abl. abs.
et tripodas geminos, auri duo magna talenta,   265
cratera antiquum quem dat Sidonia Dido.
si vero capere Italiam sceptrisque potiri
contigerit victori et praedae dicere sortem :
vidisti, quo Turnus equo, quibus ibat in armis
aureus ; ipsum illum, clipeum cristasque rubentes   270
excipiam sorti, iam nunc tua praemia, Nise.
praeterea bis sex genitor lectissima matrum
corpora captivosque dabit suaque omnibus arma ;
insuper his campi quod rex habet ipse Latinus.
te vero, mea quem spatiis propioribus aetas   275
insequitur, venerande puer, iam pectore toto
accipio et comitem casus complector in omnes.

nulla meis sine te quaeretur gloria rebus ;
seu pacem seu bella geram, tibi maxima rerum
verborumque fides.' contra quem talia fatur   280
Euryalus : ' me nulla dies tam fortibus ausis
dissimilem arguerit ; tantum fortuna secunda
haud adversa cadat. sed te super omnia dona

double accusative →unum oro : genetrix Priami de gente vetusta
est mihi, quam miseram tenuit non Ilia tellus   285
mecum excedentem, non moenia regis Acestae.
hanc ego nunc ignaram huius quodcumque pericli est
inque salutatam linquo (nox et tua testis
dextera), quod nequeam lacrimas perferre parentis.
at tu, oro, solare inopem et succurre relictae.   290
hanc sine me spem ferre tui, audentior ibo
in casus omnes.' percussa mente dedere
Dardanidae lacrimas, ante omnes pulcher Iulus,
atque animum patriae strinxit pietatis imago.

pathos- touches on emotion, → relationship with parents tum sic effatur :   *↘ impressive*   295
' sponde digna tuis ingentibus omnia coeptis.
namque erit ista mihi genetrix, nomenque Creusae
solum defuerit, nec partum gratia talem
parva manet. casus factum quicumque sequentur,
per caput hoc iuro, per quod pater ante solebat :   300
quae tibi polliceor reduci rebusque secundis,
haec eadem matrique tuae generique manebunt.'
sic ait inlacrimans ; umero simul exuit ensem
auratum, mira quem fecerat arte Lycaon
Gnosius atque habilem vagina aptarat eburna.   305
dat Niso Mnestheus pellem horrentisque leonis

exuvias, galeam fidus permutat Aletes.
protinus armati incedunt ; quos omnis euntes
primorum manus ad portas, iuvenumque senumque,
prosequitur votis.   nec non et pulcher Iulus,   310
ante annos animumque gerens curamque virilem,
multa patri mandata dabat portanda ; sed aurae
omnia discerpunt et nubibus inrita donant.

give them in vain to the clouds

The Rutulian camp through which the two Trojans make their
way is vividly described.   Nisus and Euryalus kill many a
Rutulian leader in his drunken sleep, get through the camp
and seem set on the way to success.

egressi superant fossas noctisque per umbram
castra inimica petunt, multis tamen ante futuri   315
exitio.   passim somno vinoque per herbam
corpora fusa vident, arrectos litore currus,
inter lora rotasque viros, simul arma iacere,
vina simul.   prior Hyrtacides sic ore locutus :

gerundive

' Euryale, audendum dextra ; nunc ipsa vocat res.   320
hac iter est.   tu, ne qua manus se attollere nobis
a tergo possit, custodi et consule longe ;

3 things to do:
1. act
2. keep watch

haec ego vasta dabo et lato te limite ducam.'
sic memorat vocemque premit, simul ense superbum

3. lay waste to the enemy

Rhamnetem adgreditur, qui forte tapetibus altis   325
exstructus toto proflabat pectore somnum,
rex idem et regi Turno gratissimus augur,
sed non augurio potuit depellere pestem.
tres iuxta famulos temere inter tela iacentes
armigerumque Remi premit aurigamque sub ipsis   330
nactus equis ferroque secat pendentia colla;

tum caput ipsi aufert domino truncumque relinquit
sanguine singultantem ; atro tepefacta cruore
terra torique madent. nec non Lamyrumque La-
    mumque
et iuvenem Serranum, illa qui plurima nocte   **335**
luserat, insignis facie, multoque iacebat
membra deo victus ; felix, si protinus illum
aequasset nocti ludum in lucemque tulisset.
impastus ceu plena leo per ovilia turbans
(suadet enim vesana fames) manditque trahitque   **340**
molle pecus mutumque metu, fremit ore cruento ;
nec minor Euryali caedes ; incensus et ipse
perfurit, ac multam in medio sine nomine plebem,
Fadumque Herbesumque subit Rhoetumque Aba-
    rimque
ignaros ; Rhoetum vigilantem et cuncta videntem,
sed magnum metuens se post cratera tegebat.   **346**
pectore in adverso totum cui comminus ensem
condidit adsurgenti et multa morte recepit
purpureum : vomit ille animam et cum sanguine mixta
vina refert moriens, hic furto fervidus instat.   **350**
iamque ad Messapi socios tendebat ; ibi ignem
deficere extremum et religatos rite videbat
carpere gramen equos : breviter cum talia Nisus
(sensit enim nimia caede atque cupidine ferri)
' absistamus,' ait, ' nam lux inimica propinquat.   **355**
poenarum exhaustum satis est, via facta per hostes.'
multa virum solido argento perfecta relinquunt
armaque craterasque simul pulchrosque tapetas.

Euryalus phaleras Rhamnetis et aurea bullis
cingula, Tiburti Remulo ditissimus olim   360
quae mittit dona, hospitio cum iungeret absens,
Caedicus ; ille suo moriens dat habere nepoti ;
[post mortem bello Rutuli pugnaque potiti :]
haec rapit atque umeris nequiquam fortibus aptat.
tum galeam Messapi habilem cristisque decoram   365
induit. excedunt castris et tuta capessunt. _

*Cavalry under Volcens, reinforcements for Turnus, are riding
   through the night and catch sight of the two, Euryalus being
   betrayed by the helmet of Messapus he has donned. Chal-
   lenged, they try to escape through the thick wood. Nisus
   succeeds, but not Euryalus who loses his way and is caught.
   Nisus returns to find his friend, only to witness his execution.
   He meets his own death, not before, however, he has made a
   brave effort to rescue him.*

  interea praemissi equites ex urbe Latina,
cetera dum legio campis instructa moratur,
ibant et Turno regi responsa ferebant,
ter centum, scutati omnes, Volcente magistro.   370
iamque propinquabant castris murosque subibant
cum procul hos laevo flectentes limite cernunt,
et galea Euryalum sublustri noctis in umbra
prodidit immemorem radiisque adversa refulsit.
haud temere est visum. conclamat ab agmine Vol-
     cens :   375
' state, viri. quae causa viae? quive estis in armis?
quove tenetis iter? ' nihil illi tendere contra,
sed celerare fugam in silvas et fidere nocti.
obiciunt equites sese ad divortia nota

hinc atque hinc, omnemque abitum custode coronant.
silva fuit late dumis atque ilice nigra   381
horrida, quam densi complerant undique sentes,
rara per occultos lucebat semita calles.
Euryalum tenebrae ramorum onerosaque praeda
impediunt, fallitque timor regione viarum.   385
Nisus abit ; iamque imprudens evaserat hostes
atque locos qui post Albae de nomine dicti
Albani (tum rex stabula alta Latinus habebat),
ut stetit et frustra absentem respexit amicum :
' Euryale infelix, qua te regione reliqui?   390
quave sequar?' rursus perplexum iter omne revolvens
fallacis silvae simul et vestigia retro
observata legit dumisque silentibus errat.
audit equos, audit strepitus et signa sequentum.
nec longum in medio tempus, cum clamor ad aures 395
pervenit ac videt Euryalum, quem iam manus omnis
fraude loci et noctis, subito turbante tumultu,
oppressum rapit et conantem plurima frustra.
quid faciat? qua vi iuvenem, quibus audeat armis
eripere? an sese medios moriturus in enses   400
inferat et pulchram properet per vulnera mortem?
ocius adducto torquens hastile lacerto,
suspiciens altam Lunam sic voce precatur :
' tu, dea, tu praesens nostro succurre labori,
astrorum decus et nemorum Latonia custos.   405
si qua tuis umquam pro me pater Hyrtacus aris
dona tulit, si qua ipse meis venatibus auxi
suspendive tholo aut sacra ad fastigia fixi,

[margin note: bg begins to work his way back in the darkness]

hunc sine me turbare globum et rege tela per auras.'
dixerat, et toto conixus corpore ferrum   410
conicit. hasta volans noctis diverberat umbras
et venit aversi in tergum Sulmonis ibique
frangitur, ac fisso transit praecordia ligno. → abl· abs.
volvitur ille vomens calidum de pectore flumen
frigidus et longis singultibus ilia pulsat.   415
✓ diversi circumspiciunt. hoc acrior idem
ecce aliud summa telum librabat ab aure.
dum trepidant, it hasta Tago per tempus utrumque
stridens traiectoque haesit tepefacta cerebro. → abl. abs.
saevit atrox Volcens nec teli conspicit usquam   420
auctorem, nec quo se ardens immittere possit. ← i. q.
' tu tamen interea calido mihi sanguine poenas
persolves amborum ' inquit ; simul ense recluso
ibat in Euryalum. tum vero exterritus, amens,
conclamat Nisus nec se celare tenebris   425
amplius aut tantum potuit perferre dolorem : ← anaphora
' me, me, adsum qui feci, in me convertite ferrum,
o Rutuli! mea fraus omnis, nihil iste nec ausus " iste" → Euryalus
nec potuit ; caelum hoc et conscia sidera testor '; - reasoning is that you
—tantum infelicem nimium dilexit amicum.   should attack me
                                                      430
talia dicta dabat, sed viribus ensis adactus   because he is too
transabiit costas et candida pectora rumpit. ∧ innocent
volvitur Euryalus leto, pulchrosque per artus stressing beauty and innocence
it cruor, inque umeros cervix conlapsa recumbit ; → look to Horace's poem
purpureus veluti cum flos succisus aratro   to Virgil
languescit moriens, lassove papavera collo   435
demisere caput pluvia cum forte gravantur.   - also poem to Pompeeius
                                               - from Catullus → "vivamus mea
                                                                Lesbia"

- Horace's Leuconui

at Nisus ruit in medios solumque per omnes
Volcentem petit, in solo Volcente moratur.

Nisus   → quem circum glomerati hostes hinc comminus atque
hinc   **440**
proturbant. instat non setius ac rotat ensem
fulmineum, donec Rutuli clamantis in ore
condidit adverso et moriens animam abstulit hosti.
tum super exanimum sese proiecit amicum

abl. → confossus, placidaque ibi demum morte quievit.   **445**

Virgil speaking → fortunati ambo! si quid mea carmina possunt,
nulla dies umquam memori vos eximet aevo,
dum domus Aeneae Capitoli immobile saxum
accolet imperiumque pater Romanus habebit.

victores praeda Rutuli spoliisque potiti   **450**
Volcentem exanimum flentes in castra ferebant.
nec minor in castris luctus Rhamnete reperto

dat. of reference → exsangui et primis una tot caede peremptis,

abl. abs. ⌐ Serranoque Numaque. ingens concursus ad ipsa
corpora seminecesque viros tepidaque recentem   **455**
caede locum et plenos spumanti sanguine rivos.
agnoscunt spolia inter se galeamque nitentem
Messapi et multo phaleras sudore receptas.

Turnus leads the attack on the Trojan camp, now preceded by
the grisly spectacle of the severed heads of Nisus and Euryalus.

et iam prima novo spargebat lumine terras
Tithoni croceum linquens Aurora cubile :   **460**
iam sole infuso, iam rebus luce retectis
Turnus in arma viros armis circumdatus ipse

suscitat, aeratasque acies in proelia cogit
quisque suas, variisque acuunt rumoribus iras.
quin ipsa arrectis (visu miserabile) in hastis ← *supine* **465**
praefigunt capita et multo clamore sequuntur
Euryali et Nisi. ← *half line , has not been finished*
Aeneadae duri murorum in parte sinistra
opposuere aciem (nam dextera cingitur amni)
ingentesque tenent fossas et turribus altis   **470**
stant maesti ; simul _ora_ virum praefixa movebant
_dat. → _ nota nimis _miseris_ atroque fluentia tabo.
_of
reference_

The scene inside the Trojan camp : the mother of Euryalus is seen
at her loom. Her grief, frenzy, and her laments to heaven
dismay the defenders and lower their morale.

  interea pavidam volitans pennata per urbem
nuntia Fama ruit matrisque adlabitur aures
Euryali. at subitus miserae calor ossa reliquit,   **475**
excussi manibus radii revolutaque pensa.
evolat infelix et femineo ululatu
scissa comam muros amens atque agmina cursu
prima petit, non illa virum, non illa pericli ← *syncopation*
telorumque memor, caelum dehinc questibus im-
       plet :   **480**
' hunc ego te, Euryale, aspicio? tune ille senectae
sera meae requies, potuisti linquere solam,
crudelis? nec te sub tanta pericula missum
adfari extremum miserae data copia matri?
heu, terra ignota canibus data praeda Latinis   **485**
alitibusque iaces! nec te, tua funera, mater

produxi pressive oculos aut vulnera lavi,
veste tegens tibi quam noctes festina diesque
urgebam, et telā curas solabar aniles.
quo sequar? aut quae nunc artus avulsaque membra
et funus lacerum tellus habet? hoc mihi de te,   491
nate, refers? hoc sum terraque marique secuta?
figite me, si qua est pietas, in me omnia tela
conicite, o Rutuli, me primam absumite ferro :
aut tu, magne pater divum, miserere, tuoque   495
invisum hoc detrude caput sub Tartara telo,
quando aliter nequeo crudelem abrumpere vitam.'
hoc fletu concussi animi, maestusque per omnes
it gemitus, torpent infractae ad proelia vires.

mother →illam incendentem luctus Idaeus et Actor   500
Ilionei monitu et multum lacrimantis Iuli
corripiunt interque manus sub tecta reponunt.

The attack and defence are described ; in tortoise-shell formation,
one section seeks to cross the ditch and break through—but
fails—shattered by a massive stone. Led by Mezentius and
Messapus, another group tries to fire the defensive counter-
works.

at tuba terribilem sonitum procul aere canoro
increpuit, sequitur clamor caelumque remugit.
accelerant acta pariter testudine Volsci,   505
et fossas implere parant ac vellere vallum.
quaerunt pars aditum et scalis ascendere muros,
qua rara est acies interlucetque corona
non tam spissa viris. telorum effundere contra
omne genus Teucri ac duris detrudere contis,   510

adsueti longo muros defendere bello.
saxa quoque infesto volvebant pondere, si qua
possent tectam aciem perrumpere, cum tamen omnes
ferre iuvat subter densa testudine casus.
nec iam sufficiunt. nam qua globus imminet ingens,
immanem Teucri molem volvuntque ruuntque,   516
quae stravit Rutulos late armorumque resolvit
tegmina. nec curant caeco contendere Marte
amplius audaces Rutuli, sed pellere vallo
missilibus certant.   520
parte alia horrendus visu quassabat Etruscam
pinum et fumiferos infert Mezentius ignes ;
at Messapus equum domitor, Neptunia proles,
rescindit vallum et scalas in moenia poscit.

*The poet appeals to the Muses to inspire his song, as he tells how
    Turnus leads the attack on the Trojan camp. A huge tower
    defended by the Trojans as keenly as it is attacked by the
    Italians is set on fire by Turnus, and all its defenders are lost
    except Helenor and Lycus. The former dies fighting the foe.
    The latter is caught by Turnus as he seeks the safety of the
    battlements. The attack on the camp is pressed hard and
    many heroes are slain. Ascanius in his first feat of archery
    slays Numanus, brother-in-law of Turnus, who strutting
    before the walls taunts the Trojans as he contrasts their
    effeminate dress and behaviour with the hardy training and
    education of the Italians. Ascanius' prayer to Jupiter is
    answered as he shoots and slays Numanus.*

vos, o Calliope, precor, aspirate canenti,   525
quas ibi tum ferro strages, quae funera Turnus

ediderit, quem quisque virum demiserit Orco,
et mecum ingentes oras evolvite belli.
[et meministis enim, divae, et memorare potestis.]
    turris erat vasto suspectu et pontibus altis,	530
opportuna loco, summis quam viribus omnes
expugnare Itali summaque evertere opum vi
certabant, Troës contra defendere saxis
perque cavas densi tela intorquere fenestras.
princeps ardentem coniecit lampada Turnus	535
et flammam adfixit lateri, quae plurima vento
corripuit tabulas et postibus haesit adesis.
turbati trepidare intus frustraque malorum
velle fugam. dum se glomerant retroque residunt
in partem quae peste caret, tum pondere turris	540
procubuit subito et caelum tonat omne fragore.
semineces ad terram, immani mole secuta,
confixique suis telis et pectora duro
transfossi ligno veniunt. vix unus Helenor
et Lycus elapsi ; quorum primaevus Helenor,	545
Maeonio regi quem serva Licymnia furtim
sustulerat.vetitisque ad Troiam miserat armis,
ense levis nudo parmaque inglorius alba.
isque ubi se Turni media inter milia vidit,
hinc acies atque hinc acies astare Latinas,	550
ut fera, quae densa venantum saepta corona
contra tela furit seseque haud nescia morti
inicit et saltu supra venabula fertur—
haud aliter iuvenis medios moriturus in hostes
inruit et, qua tela videt densissima, tendit.	555

at pedibus longe melior Lycus inter et hostes
inter et arma fuga muros tenet, altaque certat
prendere tecta manu sociumque attingere dextras.
quem Turnus, pariter cursu teloque secutus,
increpat his victor : ' nostrasne evadere, demens,   560
sperasti te posse manus? ' simul arripit ipsum
pendentem et magna muri cum parte revellit :
qualis ubi aut leporem aut candenti corpore cycnum
sustulit alta petens pedibus Iovis armiger uncis,
quaesitum aut matri multis balatibus agnum   565
Martius a stabulis rapuit lupus. undique clamor
tollitur ; invadunt et fossas aggere complent,
ardentes taedas alii ad fastigia iactant.
Ilioneus saxo atque ingenti fragmine montis
Lucetium portae subeuntem ignesque ferentem,   570
Emathiona Liger, Corynaeum sternit Asilas,
hic iaculo bonus, hic longe fallente sagitta ;
Ortygium Caeneus, victorem Caenea Turnus,
Turnus Ityn Cloniumque, Dioxippum Promolumque
et Sagarim et summis stantem pro turribus Idan,   575
Privernum Capys. hunc primo levis hasta Themillae
strinxerat, ille manum proiecto tegmine demens
ad vulnus tulit ; ergo alis adlapsa sagitta,
et laevo infixa est lateri manus, abditaque intus
spiramenta animae letali vulnere rupit.   580
stabat in egregiis Arcentis filius armis
pictus acu chlamydem et ferrugine clarus Hibera,
insignis facie, genitor quem miserat Arcens,
eductum Martis luco Symaethia circum

flumina, pinguis ubi et placabilis ara Palici :   585
stridentem fundam positis Mezentius hastis
ipse ter adducta circum caput egit habena
et media adversi liquefacto tempora plumbo
diffidit, ac multa porrectum extendit harena.

    tum primum bello celerem intendisse sagittam   590
dicitur ante feras solitus terrere fugaces
Ascanius, fortemque manu fudisse Numanum,
cui Remulo cognomen erat, Turnique minorem
germanam nuper thalamo sociatus habebat.
is primam ante aciem digna atque indigna relatu   595
vociferans tumidusque novo praecordia regno
ibat et ingentem sese clamore ferebat :
' non pudet obsidione iterum valloque teneri,
bis capti Phryges, et morti praetendere muros?
en qui nostra sibi bello conubia poscunt!   600
quis deus Italiam, quae vos dementia adegit?
non hic Atridae nec fandi fictor Ulixes :
durum ab stirpe genus natos ad flumina primum
deferimus saevoque gelu duramus et undis ;
venatu invigilant pueri silvasque fatigant ;   605
flectere ludus equos et spicula tendere cornu.
at patiens operum parvoque adsueta iuventus
aut rastris terram domat aut quatit oppida bello.
omne aevum ferro teritur, versaque iuvencum
terga fatigamus hasta, nec tarda senectus   610
debilitat vires animi mutatque vigorem :
canitiem galea premimus, semperque recentes
comportare iuvat praedas et vivere rapto.

vobis picta croco et fulgenti murice vestis,
desidiae cordi, iuvat indulgere choreis,   615
et tunicae manicas et habent redimicula mitrae.
o vere Phrygiae, neque enim Phryges, ite per alta
Dindyma, ubi adsuetis biforem dat tibia cantum.
tympana vos buxusque vocat Berecyntia Matris
Idaeae, sinite arma viris et cedite ferro.'   620
    talia iactantem dictis ac dira canentem
non tulit Ascanius, nervoque obversus equino
intendit telum diversaque bracchia ducens
constitit, ante Iovem supplex per vota precatus :
' Iuppiter omnipotens, audacibus adnue coeptis.   625
ipse tibi ad tua templa feram sollemnia dona,
et statuam ante aras aurata fronte iuvencum
candentem pariterque caput cum matre ferentem,
iam cornu petat et pedibus qui spargat harenam.'
audiit et caeli genitor de parte serena   630
intonuit laevum, sonat una fatifer arcus.
effugit horrendum stridens adducta sagitta
perque caput Remuli venit et cava tempora ferro
traicit. ' i, verbis virtutem inlude superbis!   634
bis capti Phryges haec Rutulis responsa remittunt.'
hoc tantum Ascanius. Teucri clamore sequuntur
laetitiaque fremunt animosque ad sidera tollunt.

VERGIL

*Apollo who is watching from the heavens congratulates Ascanius
and prophesies the greatness of his race. Then assuming the
shape of the aged Butes, he tells him to withdraw from the
fighting. The Trojans, recognising the presence of the god
from the rattle of his quiver, keep Ascanius from the battle
which they then renew with great ferocity.*

aetheria tum forte plaga crinitus Apollo
desuper Ausonias acies urbemque videbat,
nube sedens, atque his victorem adfatur Iulum : 640
' macte nova virtute, puer, sic itur ad astra,
dis genite et geniture deos. iure omnia bella
gente sub Assaraci fato ventura resident,
nec te Troia capit.' simul haec effatus ab alto
aethere se mittit, spirantes dimovet auras 645
Ascaniumque petit. formam tum vertitur oris
antiquum in Buten. hic Dardanio Anchisae
armiger ante fuit fidusque ad limina custos ;
tum comitem Ascanio pater addidit. ibat Apollo
omnia longaevo similis, vocemque coloremque 650
et crines albos et saeva sonoribus arma,
atque his ardentem dictis adfatur Iulum :
' sit satis, Aenide, telis impune Numanum
oppetiisse tuis ; primam hanc tibi magnus Apollo
concedit laudem et paribus non invidet armis ; 655
cetera parce, puer, bello.' sic orsus Apollo
mortales medio aspectus sermone reliquit
et procul in tenuem ex oculis evanuit auram.
agnovere deum proceres divinaque tela
Dardanidae pharetramque fuga sensere sonantem. 660
ergo avidum pugnae dictis ac numine Phoebi

Ascanium prohibent, ipsi in certamina rursus
succedunt animasque in aperta pericula mittunt.
it clamor totis per propugnacula muris,
intendunt acres arcus amentaque torquent.   665
sternitur omne solum telis, tum scuta cavaeque
dant sonitum flictu galeae, pugna aspera surgit :
quantus ab occasu veniens pluvialibus Haedis
verberat imber humum, quam multa grandine nimbi
in vada praecipitant, cum Iuppiter horridus austris
torquet aquosam hiemem et caelo cava nubila rumpit.

*The Trojans Pandarus and Bitias open the camp gates to make
a sally but actually admit the Rutulians who force their way
in amid fierce fighting.*

Pandarus et Bitias, Idaeo Alcanore creti,   672
quos Iovis eduxit luco silvestris Iaera
abietibus iuvenes patriis et montibus aequos,
portam, quae ducis imperio commissa, recludunt   675
freti armis, ultroque invitant moenibus hostem.
ipsi intus dextra ac laeva pro turribus astant,
armati ferro et cristis capita alta corusci :
quales aëriae liquentia flumina circum
sive Padi ripis Athesim seu propter amoenum   680
consurgunt geminae quercus intonsaque caelo
attollunt capita et sublimi vertice nutant.
inrumpunt aditus Rutuli ut videre patentes.
continuo Quercens et pulcher Aquiculus armis
et praeceps animi Tmarus et Mavortius Haemon   685
agminibus totis aut versi terga dedere

aut ipso portae posuere in limine vitam.
tum magis increscunt animis discordibus irae,
et iam collecti Troës glomerantur eodem
et conferre manum et procurrere longius audent.   690

At news of this, Turnus arrives and makes great slaughter among
the Trojans, killing Bitias.

  ductori Turno diversa in parte furenti
turbantique viros perfertur nuntius, hostem
fervere caede nova et portas praebere patentes.
deserit inceptum atque immani concitus ira
Dardaniam ruit ad portam fratresque superbos.   695
et primum Antiphaten (is enim se primus agebat),
Thebana de matre nothum Sarpedonis alti,
coniecto sternit iaculo ; volat Itala cornus
aëra per tenerum stomachoque infixa sub altum
pectus abit : reddit specus atri vulneris undam   700
spumantem, et fixo ferrum in pulmone tepescit.
tum Meropem atque Erymanta manu, tum sternit
    Aphidnum,
tum Bitian ardentem oculis animisque frementem,
non iaculo (neque enim iaculo vitam ille dedisset),
sed magnum stridens contorta phalarica venit,   705
fulminis acta modo, quam nec duo taurea terga,
nec duplici squama lorica fidelis et auro
sustinuit ; conlapsa ruunt immania membra.
dat tellus gemitum, et clipeum super intonat ingens.
talis in Euboico Baiarum litore quondam   710
saxea pila cadit, magnis quam molibus ante

constructam ponto iaciunt, sic illa ruinam
prona trahit penitusque vadis inlisa recumbit ;
miscent se maria et nigrae attolluntur harenae,
tum sonitu Prochyta alta tremit durumque cubile   715
Inarime Iovis imperiis imposta Typhoeo.

*With a mighty effort Pandarus manages to close the gate but finds
to his horror that he has shut in (like a tiger among the herds)
the Rutulian leader. His spear deflected by Juno misses its
target and he is slain by Turnus.*

hic Mars armipotens animum viresque Latinis
addidit et stimulos acres sub pectore vertit,
immisitque Fugam Teucris atrumque Timorem.
undique conveniunt, quoniam data copia pugnae,   720
bellatorque animo deus incidit.
Pandarus, ut fuso germanum corpore cernit
et quo sit fortuna loco, qui casus agat res,
portam vi multa converso cardine torquet,
obnixus latis umeris, multosque suorum   725
moenibus exclusos duro in certamine linquit ;
ast alios secum includit recipitque ruentes,
demens, qui Rutulum in medio non agmine regem
viderit inrumpentem ultroque incluserit urbi,
immanem veluti pecora intei inertia tigrim.   730
continuo nova lux oculis effulsit, et arma
horrendum sonuere, tremunt in vertice cristae
sanguineae clipeoque micantia fulmina mittit.
agnoscunt faciem invisam atque immania membra
turbati subito Aeneadae. tum Pandarus ingens   735

emicat et mortis fraternae fervidus ira
effatur : ' non haec dotalis regia Amatae ;
nec muris cohibet patriis media Ardea Turnum.
castra inimica vides, nulla hinc exire potestas.'
olli subridens sedato pectore Turnus :   740
' incipe, si qua animo virtus, et consere dextram :
hic etiam inventum Priamo narrabis Achillem.'
dixerat. ille rudem nodis et cortice crudo
intorquet summis adnixus viribus hastam ;
excepere aurae, vulnus Saturnia Iuno   745
detorsit veniens, portaeque infigitur hasta.
' at non hoc telum, mea quod vi dextera versat,
effugies, neque enim is teli nec vulneris auctor.'
sic ait et sublatum alte consurgit in ensem
et mediam ferro gemina inter tempora frontem   750
dividit impubesque immani vulnere malas.
fit sonus, ingenti concussa est pondere tellus ;·
conlapsos artus atque arma cruenta cerebro
sternit humi moriens, atque illi partibus aequis
huc caput atque illuc umero ex utroque pependit.   755

*The Trojans panic and Turnus in his lust for blood misses his
opportunity to throw open the gates to his men outside.
Instead, carried away, he deals death blows all around him.*

diffugiunt versi trepida formidine Troës.
et si continuo victorem ea cura subisset,
rumpere claustra manu sociosque immittere portis,
ultimus ille dies bello gentique fuisset,

sed furor ardentem caedisque insana cupido   760
egit in adversos.
principio Phalerim et succiso poplite Gygen
excipit, hinc raptas fugientibus ingerit hastas
in tergus, Iuno vires animumque ministrat.
addit Halyn comitem et confixa Phegea parma,   765
ignaros deinde in muris Martemque cientes
Alcandrumque Haliumque Noëmonaque Prytanimque.
Lyncea tendentem contra sociosque vocantem
vibranti gladio conixus ab aggere dexter
occupat, huic uno deiectum comminus ictu   770
cum galea longe iacuit caput. inde ferarum
vastatorem Amycum, quo non felicior alter
ungere tela manu ferrumque armare veneno,
et Clytium Aeoliden et amicum Crethea Musis,
Crethea Musarum comitem, cui carmina semper   775
et citharae cordi numerosque intendere nervis,
semper equos atque arma virum pugnasque canebat.

*At last the leaders Mnestheus and Serestus rally the Trojans
and drive Turnus back like a lion at bay. Now hard pressed
and overwhelmed by Trojan missiles and spears, the Rutulian
hero has to seek safety by plunging into the Tiber.*

tandem ductores audita caede suorum
conveniunt Teucri, Mnestheus acerque Serestus,
palantesque vident socios hostemque receptum.   780
et Mnestheus : ' quo deinde fugam, quo tenditis? ' inquit.
' quos alios muros, quae iam ultra moenia habetis?
unus homo et vestris, o cives, undique saeptus

aggeribus tantas strages impune per urbem
ediderit? iuvenum primos tot miserit Orco?   785
non infelicis patriae veterumque deorum
et magni Aeneae, segnes, miseretque pudetque? '
talibus accensi firmantur et agmine denso
consistunt. Turnus paulatim excedere pugna
et fluvium petere ac partem quae cingitur unda.   790
acrius hoc Teucri clamore incumbere magno
et glomerare manum, ceu saevum turba leonem
cum telis premit infensis ; at territus ille,
asper, acerba tuens, retro redit, et neque terga
ira dare aut virtus patitur, nec tendere contra   795
ille quidem hoc cupiens potis est per tela virosque.
haud aliter retro dubius vestigia Turnus
improperata refert et mens exaestuat ira.
quin etiam bis tum medios invaserat hostes,
bis confusa fuga per muros agmina vertit ;   800
sed manus e castris propere coït omnis in unum,
nec contra vires audet Saturnia Iuno
sufficere ; aëriam caelo nam Iuppiter Irim
demisit germanae haud mollia iussa ferentem,
ni Turnus cedat Teucrorum moenibus altis.   805
ergo nec clipeo iuvenis subsistere tantum
nec dextra valet, iniectis sic undique telis
obruitur. strepit adsiduo cava tempora circum
tinnitu galea et saxis solida aera fatiscunt,
discussaeque iubae capiti, nec sufficit umbo   810

ictibus ; ingeminant hastis et Troës et ipse
fulmineus Mnestheus. tum toto corpore sudor
liquitur et piceum (nec respirare potestas)
flumen agit, fessos quatit aeger anhelitus artus.
tum demum praeceps saltu sese omnibus armis   815
in fluvium dedit. ille suo cum gurgite flavo
accepit venientem ac mollibus extulit undis
et laetum sociis abluta caede remisit.

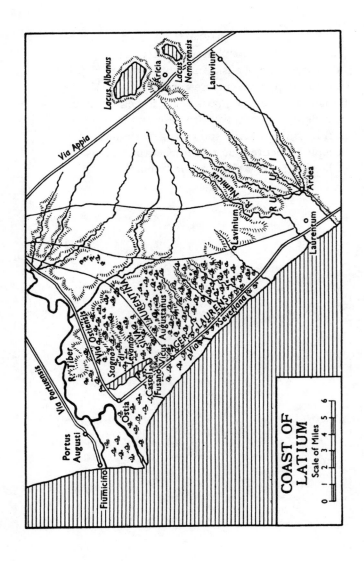

COAST OF LATIUM

Scale of Miles

0 1 2 3 4 5 6

NOTES

Line 1. **ea** is nom. pl. neuter and the subject of **geruntur.**
Begin the line with **atque dum** and note that the conjunction
has the present tense even when the main verb is in the past :
' and while such (deeds) were happening . . . '. For the events
of Book VIII, see the Introduction, p. xvii. **penitus** goes with
diversa parte, ' in far distant parts '. Note the absence of the
preposition **in,** a very common omission in Latin poetry with
the abl. of place where, (local abl.).

l. 2. **Irim.** **Iris,** the goddess of the rainbow, was often used
by Juno as her messenger. The beginner should note that such
intervention as this on the part of the gods and goddesses is an
important part of the epic convention.

Saturnia Juno. Throughout the Aeneid Juno pursues the
Trojans and their leader Aeneas with implacable hatred. The
prime cause of this bitter feeling against them was no doubt the
judgment that Paris made when he was called on to award the
golden apple to the most beautiful of the goddesses, an honour
claimed by Juno, Venus and Minerva. All three competitors
attempted to bribe the judge, and Paris gave the prize to
Venus, who had promised him the lovely Helen, wife of the
Greek king Menelaus.

In Book I, ll. 25 sqq., Vergil describes her anger : ' and not
even yet had the cause of her anger and her cruel resentment
faded from her heart : there remains hidden away deep in her
mind the judgment of Paris and the insult of her beauty scorned. '.

> **necdum etiam causae irarum saevique dolores**
> **exciderant animo ; manet alta mente repostum**
> **iudicium Paridis spretaequ' iniuria formae.**

l. 3. **ad Turnum.** For the part played in Vergil's epic by
Turnus, chieftain of the Rutuli and leader of the native opposi-
tion to Aeneas, see the Introduction, p. xvii.

luco = in luco. See the note above on l. 1. Similarly,
sacrata valle in the next line.

l. 4. **Pilumni.** Pilumnus was a mythical ancestor of Turnus. **parentis,** therefore =' forefather ', ' forbear '.

l. 5. **ad quem.** It is unnatural in English to use the relative pronoun after a major stop. This Latin idiom, known as relative connection, is best turned into English by personal or demonstrative pronouns. Hence render : ' to him '. **Thaumantias,** *lit.* ' daughter of Thaumas ', i.e. Iris. Thaumas, is a Greek name meaning ' wonderful ' ; he was son of Ocean and Earth.

ll. 6, 7. **quod . . . ultro,** ' what to (thee) praying no one of the gods would dare to promise, lo! rolling time has brought unasked.'

Note : (i) ' to thee praying ' =' to thy prayers '. (ii) **divum** is gen. pl. This ending was actually the original termination of the 2nd declension before it was ousted by -**orum** on the analogy of the 1st decl. -**arum** and it is often found in poetry. (iii) **volvenda dies** ; the gerundive has here the force of an *intransitive* present participle **volvens.** (iv) **ultro** is always used of going *beyond* what is normally expected. Its translation depends upon the context : here ' unasked ' or ' unbidden ' will do.

l. 8. **urbe.** By ' city ' Vergil means here the settlement, half-town, half-camp, which Aeneas had built near the mouth of the Tiber. This is the camp of Aeneas which is situated within sight of the sea, not far from the Tiber's mouth on the south bank of the river. In fact, as we learn later, it is bounded on one side by the river.

l. 9. **sceptra\ Palatini,** ' the kingdom of the Palatine '. **sceptra** is pl. for sg., and the Palatine is the hill of that name on which Evander had built his town Pallanteum. **Euandri.** See the Introduction, p. xvii. **petit** : present. Note that the final syllable, though naturally short, is lengthened by ictus or the stress. The fifth foot is a spondee.

l. 10. **extremas ad Corythi urbes,** ' to the furthest cities of Corynthus '. As the latter was believed to be the founder of an Etruscan city, ' of Corythus ' =' of Etruria '.

l. 11. **Lydorum . . . agrestes,** 'and he is arming the band of the Lydians, country-folk whom he has mustered.'

Note : (i) **Lydorum** = **Etruscorum,** for Etruria was believed by the ancients to have been colonised from Lydia in Asia Minor. (ii) **collectos agrestes,** *lit.,* 'the having been mustered country-folk ' is in apposition with **manum.**

l. 12. **nunc . . . currus.** Supply **est. Currus** is acc. pl.

l. 13. **turbata . . . castra,** *lit.,* ' seize the surprised camp ', is the natural Latin for ' surprise and seize the camp '. In fact, when a subject has two verbs, it is perhaps more usual to express the first of the two actions by a perfect participle passive, here in agreement with the direct object. Cf. **nuntium captum interfecerunt,** normal Latin for ' they caught and killed the messenger '.

l. 14. **paribus alis,** ' on equal (i.e. poised) wings '. **sustulit** from **tollo.**

l. 15. **fuga,** abl. as the scansion shows. The line will be easily understood if it is remembered that the track of Iris' flight through the heavens is marked by a rainbow.

l. 17. **ac . . . secutus,** ' and with such words pursued (her) fleeing (= her in her flight) '.

l. 18. **decus caeli,** ' glory of the sky ' is in apposition with **Iri,** vocative. **quis . . . in terras,** ' who brought thee down to me, sent from heaven (*lit.,* from the clouds) to earth '.

ll. 18, 19. **unde . . . tempestas,** ' whence this so clear weather suddenly '. ' clear weather ' = ' brightness in the sky ' : thus we get : ' whence this sudden brightness in the sky? '

ll. 20, 21. **medium . . . stellas,** ' I see the heavens rent asunder (*lit.,* part in-the-middle) and the stars wandering in the firmament '.

l. 22. **quisquis . . . vocas,** ' whoever thou (art that) summonest (me) to battle '. Turnus has recognised Iris but does not know which of the gods has sent her to him with her message.

l. 23. **summo de gurgite,** ' from the surface of the water '.
ad undam in the previous line means of course ' to the river ',
i.e. the Tiber. He needed water to wash his hands in purifica-
tion before he prayed.

l. 24. **multa,** acc. pl. neuter of the adj. used adverbially with
orans, ' with many a prayer to ' : *lit.,* ' praying much to '.
aethera. The -a ending is that of the acc. sing. in the Greek
3rd declension and is often used by Vergil in words derived
from Greek.

l. 25. **campis apertis,** ' on the . . . ' : local abl. without a
preposition.

l. 26. **dives equum . . .,** ' rich *in* horses, rich *in* . . .'.

Note : (i) **equum,** gen. pl. See l. 6. (ii) the gen. after **dives** :
this case is that normally found after words denoting ' full-
ness '. (iii) **pictai,** three syllables, is an old form of the gen. sg.

l. 27. **primas acies,** ' the van '. Messapus was the leader of
a contingent from Southern Etruria. **postrema,** acc. pl. neut.,
' the rear '.

l. 28. **Tyrrhidae iuvenes,** nom. pl. ' the young sons of
Tyrrhus '. The latter was the chief herdsman of Latinus, the
Latin king.

medio . . . Turnus, ' Turnus (is) leader in the middle '.

l. 29. **vertitur . . . est.** This line, which is omitted by all good
manuscripts because it has probably been introduced from
Book VII, 784, can be ignored.

ll. 30–32. **ceu . . . alveo,** ' even as Ganges in silence rising
high with his seven peaceful streams or the Nile when with its
rich flood it flows back from the fields and has by now sunk
within its (proper) channel '.

Elaborate similes are an essential feature of the epic tradition
and at times seem very artificial and strained to modern
readers. Here Vergil compares the silent march of the host
of Turnus to the regular rise and fall of the two great rivers.
Note that he gives to the Ganges the seven mouths and annual

overflow of the Nile. Romans had, of course, only very hazy
ideas of the geography of the East.

alveo is scanned as two syllables.

l. 33. **nigro pulvere** is abl. of description, which always
consists of two words, noun and adjective, and is equivalent to
an English phrase with ' of '.

l. 34. **campis,** ' on the plains ', local abl. again.

l. 35. **ab adversa mole,** ' from the rampart facing (the foe) '.
Caicus, three syllables. **prospiciunt, conclamat.** The begin-
ner will have noticed the sudden use of the present : this may
be regarded as an instance of the historic present and trans-
lated accordingly as a past, or the tense of the Latin may be
retained in translation, even though at times Vergil uses now
past, now present, with great freedom.

l. 36. **caligine atra,** ' in murky gloom '. **volvitur.** See the
note on l. 414.

l. 37. **citi,** adj. for adv. ; hence ' quickly '.

l. 39. **per omnes . . . portas,** ' the Trojans hide themselves
(i.e. take refuge) through all the gates '. As in the next words
we learn that ' they man the walls ', Vergil must be referring to
those Trojans outside the fortified camp.

l. 40. **discedens,** *lit.,* ' departing ', i.e. ' on his departure '.

optimus armis Aeneas, ' Aeneas best in arms ', i.e. ' A.,
noblest of warriors '. **armis** is an abl. of respect.

ll. 41–43. **si qua . . . muros,** ' if any crisis meanwhile arose,
they were not to venture to draw up their line nor trust the
field ; they were only to keep safe their camp and walls, pro-
tected (**tutos**) by their rampart '.

Note : (i) **qua,** indefinite adj., ' any ', always found after **si,
nisi, num, ne.** (ii) **fuisset** represents the future-perfect of direct
speech. (iii) **auderent, servarent,** subj. in indirect command.

l. 44. **monstrat** is singular although it has two subjects,
pudor, ira. The verb has an unusual meaning, ' prompt ' *or*
' encourage ' and is followed by the infinitive. In prose, verbs
of such meaning would have **ut** + subjunctive.

l. 45. **facessunt** is another form of **faciunt**.

l. 46. **cavis turribus**, local abl. ; ' within their hollow (i.e. the protection of) towers '.

l. 47. **ut** with the indicative means ' as ' or ' when ', the former here. **ante** is an adverb.

l. 48. **viginti . . . comitatus.** The participle **comitatus** (from the deponent **comitor**) has a passive meaning : the omission of the preposition **a** with **viginti lectis** is poetic as is the partitive gen. **equitum** ; prose would have **equitibus.** et links the two verbs **praecesserat** and **adest** in the subordinate clause **ut . . . adest. urbi** is dat. with **adest**, ' is upon the city '.

l. 49. **quem**, relative connection, ' him '. See l. 5.

ll. 49, 50. **maculis Thracius albis equus**, ' a white-spotted Thracian steed '. **crista rubra** is abl. Supply ' him ' as the object of **tegit.**

l. 51. **ecquis erit, iuvenes . . .** ' will there be anyone, warriors . . .? '

l. 52. **emittit.** Supply ' it ', i.e. the javelin as the object. **in auras**, ' into the breezes ', i.e. ' into the heavens '.

l. 53. **principium (pugnae)** is accus. in apposition to the previous sentence—' the beginning of battle '. **et campo . . . infert**, ' and stalks (head on) high o'er the plain '. **se inferre** is often used in the meaning : ' enter ', ' advance ', ' move '.

l. 55. **Teucrum**, gen. pl. **mirantur** has dependent upon it : (i) direct object, **inertia corda** (ii) three accusatives and infinitives, **(eos) non dare se campo . . . fovere.**

Note : (i) **non dare se** (with **eos** as the subject to be supplied) : ' that they do not entrust themselves '. Cf. l. 42. (ii) **non . . . fovere**, ' that they do not bear arms against (the foes) like heroes **(viros)** but hug their camp '.

l. 57. **huc atque huc**, ' here and there '. **turbidus**, adj. for adv., ' wildly '.

l. 58. **equo**, ' on horseback '. **per avia**, ' where way is none ' is Conington's happy translation.

ll. 59–61. **ac veluti . . . media.** Order for translation : **ac veluti cum lupus insidiatus pleno ovili fremit ad caulas super media nocte, perpessus ventos et imbres.**

Note : (i) **insidiatus, perpessus.** The perfect participle of deponent verbs is often equivalent to the English *present* participle. (ii) **super . . . nocte,** ' at midnight '—metrical reasons alone must explain this use of **super** with the abl., especially as the abl. alone expresses ' time when '.

l. 62. **balatum exercent,** ' keep bleating '. **improbus,** a favourite adjective with Vergil which means ' persistent beyond reason '. ı

l. 63. **saevit in absentes,** ' rages against the absent ones ', i.e. ' against those he cannot reach '.

ll. 63–64. **collecta . . . fauces,** *lit.,* 'the long-gathered (**ex longo collecta**) fury of eating and his jaws dry from blood goad (him) '. If we render ' of eating ' by ' of hunger ' and ' jaws dry from blood ' by ' blood-parched jaws ', and finally turn the sentence into the passage, we get : ' goaded by the long-gathered fury of hunger and by his . . .'. **sanguine** is an abl. of separation after **siccae.**

l. 65. **haud aliter,** ' not otherwise ' = 'even so '. **Rutulo tuenti,** dat. of the person interested : but translate ' as the Rutulian (i.e. Turnus) gazed upon '.

l. 66. **duris ossibus,** ' in his iron frame '.

ll. 67–68. **qua . . . in aequor,** ' by what means is he to try entrance? what course is to hurl the imprisoned Trojans from the rampart and fling them on the plain? ' Note the delibera-tive subjunctives, employed when one ponders the wisdom of a course of action.

ll. 69–71. **classem . . . invadit.** The order of the Latin may be retained if it is remembered that **classem** is acc., object of **invadit. saeptam** is in agreement with it.

l. 71. **sociosque . . . ovantes.** Note the double acc. after **poscit.**

incendia is plural for sing.

l. 73. **incumbunt,** ' they set to work '. **urget praesentia Turni** would be more natural in the passive in English : ' encouraged by the presence of T.'

l. 74. **accingitur.** The Latin passive occasionally has the meaning of the active used reflexively : hence **accingitur = se accingit.**

l. 75. **diripuere.** The perfect tense, introduced here among so many verbs in the present, expresses rapidity or suddenness of action : ' at once they have plundered the hearths ', i.e. for fire. **fert** has two subjects : (i) **fumida taeda,** sg. for pl., ' smoking brands ' and (ii) **Volcanus,** ' the god of fire ' who is used for the object of which he is the tutelary deity. With the first, the verb means ' gives forth ', with the second ' rolls '. **commixtam favillam,** *lit.,* ' ash mingled ' i.e. (with fire and smoke). Translate : ' clouds of sooty smoke '.

l. 77. **Teucris,** abl. of separation, ' from the Trojans '. This invocation of the Muses may seem very artificial to the modern reader, but it is an essential feature of the epic tradition.

l. 78. **avertit,** perfect. **ratibus,** abl., ' from the ships '.

l. 79. **prisca . . . perennis,** *lit.,* ' belief in the deed (is) old but its fame (is) everlasting.'

ll. 80, 81. **tempore quo,** ' at the time at which ', i.e. ' at the time when '. **Phrygia in Ida.** The latter, a mountain near Troy, was greatly celebrated in Greek, and therefore, in Latin poetry. It was here, we are told, that Paris judged the well-known contest of the three goddesses. See note on l. 2. **pelagi alta. alta** is acc. pl. neuter and **pelagi** is the gen. of the divided whole (partitive) : = ' the deep sea '.

l. 82. **genetrix Berecyntia,** ' the Berecyntian mother ' is Cybele, an eastern mother-goddess with whom Vergil identifies Rhea, the mother of Jupiter. Berecyntus is a mountain in Phrygia, sacred to Cybele. In the illustration on p. 7, the goddess is represented with a walled crown as city goddess. **fertur adfata,** ' is said to have addressed '.

l. 83. **petenti,** ' to (me) entreating ', i.e. ' to my entreaty '.

l. 84. **domito Olympo,** ' Olympus conquered ', abl. absol. i.e.
' after thy conquest of O.' There is a legend that Cybele or
rather Rhea prevented her husband Chronos[1] from devouring
his son Zeus[2] when a baby. Now that he has overthrown his
father and become king of the Olympian gods, he has the power
not only to grant her request but also to make her some
recompense.

ll. 85–87. **pinea . . . acernis,** ' there is to me (=I have) a
forest of pine, beloved for many years ; a grove was on the
mountain-top to which (**quo**) (men) brought offerings, shaded
with black firs and trunks of maple '.

l. 88. **Dardanio iuveni,** i.e. Aeneas. **Dardanius =** ' Trojan '
often occurs in the Aeneid. The adjective is derived from
Dardanus, an ancestor of the Trojans. **classis** is gen. after
egeret, a verb which may govern that case as well as the abl.

l. 89. **laeta,** adj. for adv., ' joyfully '. **nunc . . . angit,** ' now
anxious fear constrains (me) troubled ' = ' my troubled
heart '.

l. 90. **solve . . . parentem,** ' loose (my) fears and let a mother
(**parentem**) have this power (**hoc posse**) by her prayers '.

l. 91. **quassatae,** perf. part. passive, agrees with the subject
of **vincantur, trabes,** ' timbers ', i.e. the ship. Translate as if
you had **quatiantur et vincantur. cursu ullo,** ' by any voyage '.

l. 92. **prosit . . . ortas,** *lit.,* ' let it be an advantage that they
were born upon my hills ' : i.e. ' let their birth upon my hills
be a boon to them '.

l. 93. **contra,** ' in reply ', with which ' said ' has to be
supplied.

l. 94. **istis,** either ' for those (ships) of thine ' or ' by such
(prayers) of thine '.

ll. 95–97. **mortaline . . . potestas,** ' are ships made by mortal
hand to possess immortal rights? Is Aeneas to pass through
dangers uncertain, certain (of his goal)? To what god was
power so great entrusted? '

[1] In Latin, Saturnus.
[2] In Latin, Jupiter.

Note : (i) **habeant, lustret,** deliberative subjunctives. (ii) the effective contrast of **mortali, immortale ; certus, incerta.**

l. 98. **defunctae,** note the gender, fem. The perf. part., therefore, agrees with ' the ships' (understood); ' having fulfilled (their task) '.

l. 99. **Ausonios.** The adj. **Ausonius** is derived from Ausones or Ausonii, an ancient name for the people of Southern Italy : hence it means ' Italian'. Here the adj. agrees with **portus,** acc. pl.

ll. 99–101. **quaecumque . . . eripiam formam.** In this sentence we have a common Latin idiom : the relative clause preceding the main one and the antecedent being omitted. Supply ' from each one ' before **quaecumque.**

Note also : (i) **evaserit, vexerit** are future-perfect in accordance with Latin idiom which is more precise in its use of tenses in subordinate clauses when the main verb is future. We use the present. (ii) **Laurentia arva,** ' to the Laurentian fields', acc. of the goal of motion. In prose **ad** would be necessary. ' Laurentian ' = ' Latin ', for Laurentum was an old Latin town by the sea, the capital of the king of Latium, Latinus.

l. 102. **quales Nereia Doto et Galatea secant,** ' even as Doto daughter of Nereus and Galatea cleave '. **pectore,** sg, for pl., ' with their breasts '. **Nereus** was a sea-deity, father of the sea-nymphs, the Nereids. **tales** has to be supplied as the antecedent of **quales,** *lit.,* ' such as '.

l. 104. **dixerat,** ' he had spoken ', = ' he ceased '.

ll. 104–106. **idque . . . adnuit.** Order for translation : **-que per flumina Stygii fratris** (i.e. Pluto), **per ripas torrentes pice atraque voragine adnuit id ratum.** The last three words mean *lit.,* ' he nodded it confirmed ', i.e. ' he confirmed (his promise) and nodded (his assent) '.

The Styx was one of the rivers of Hades and the oath upon its waters was the most solemn that the gods could use. Cf. Vergil VI, l. 324 : ' . . . and the Stygian mere, by whose divinity the gods fear to swear falsely '.

... Stygiamque paludem,
di cuius iurare timent et fallere numen.

l. 108. debita, *lit.*, ' owed ' = ' due ', ' appointed '.
complerant = **compleverant.** In verb forms containing the letter v, that and the following vowel often disappear in what are known as syncopated forms. **Matrem** is the ' mother-goddess ', i.e. Cybele.

Turni iniuria. Turni is subjective gen., ' the wrong done by Turnus '. **admonuit** is here followed by the simple infin. **depellere** : in prose **ut** with the subjunctive would be necessary. **ratibus sacris,** ' from her sacred ships '.

l. 110. hic, adv., ' hereupon '. **nova lux,** ' a strange light '. The appearance of the goddess is naturally accompanied by a strange radiance and other wonders.

l. 111. visus. Supply **est.**

l. 112. Idaeique chori, ' and the troops of Ida '. This phrase is also the subject of **visus transcurrere.** Its position at the end of the sentence, however, is awkward and perhaps we might say : ' and Ida's troops were in attendance '.

' The troops of Ida ' are the Corybantes, attendants of the mother-goddess Cybele on Mount Ida near Troy ; a feature of their worship was the use of cymbal and dance to arouse religious frenzy.

l. 114. ne trepidate. ne or **nec** with the imperative is often used in verse where in prose we should find **noli** with the present infinitive : ' be not anxious '.

ll. 115, 116. maria . . . pinus, ' it shall be granted to Turnus to burn up the seas sooner than my sacred pines '.

solutae. Note the gender which shows that Cybele is addressing the ships : ' loosed ', i.e. ' free '.

l. 117. sua quaeque. Sua goes with **vincula, quaeque** with **puppes.** The latter equals ' ships ', being an instance of the part being used for the whole, *synecdoche.* Latin is fond of this juxtaposition of **quisque** with **suus.**

l. 118. ripis, ' from the bank '.

l. 119. **delphinum modo,** ' in the manner of dolphins ', i.e.
' like dolphins '. **demersis rostris.** Read the note on l. 13 and
translate as if you had : **rostra demergunt et petunt.**

ll. 120–122. **hinc . . . feruntur,** ' then (as) the forms of
maidens (**virgineae facies**)—a wonderful portent—they return
(from the depths) and move o'er the sea in like number
(**totidem**) as before they had stood on the shore (as) bronze-
beaked prows '.

Line 121 is omitted by the best manuscripts and is, therefore,
regarded as being an interpolation from Book X, 223.

Note : the passive of **fero** used almost as a deponent, ' I
move ', ' go ', ' sail ', etc.

l. 123. **animis,** ' in their hearts ', either a locative or a local
abl. without a preposition.

l. 124. **turbatis equis,** ' his steeds being confused ', abl. absol.
Messapus is riding a chariot, of course.

ll. 124, 125. **cunctatur . . . ab alto,** ' and the stream Tiberi-
nus with its hoarse sound tarries and recalls its step from the
deep '. Even the river is affected ; it stands still, so to speak,
and ceases to flow into the sea. **rauca sonans,** *lit.,* ' sounding
hoarse ' : the acc. pl. neuter of the adj. being used adverbially.

l. 126. **at . . . cessit,** ' but confidence did not withdraw from
reckless T.' i.e. ' reckless T. did not lose his confidence '. Note
the picture we get here of the Rutulian leader : a fearless single-
minded warrior who cares not for omens or portents but has one
purpose which he pursues ruthlessly—the destruction of the
hated invader.

l. 127. **ultro,** ' nay more '. See the note on ll. 6, 7. The
second **ultro** may be rendered by ' actually '.

l. 128. **Troianos . . . petunt.** Note the emphatic position of
Troianos : ' (it is) the Trojans these portents attack '. **his,**
' from them ', the usual dat. found after compound verbs.

ll. 129, 130. **non . . . Rutulos,** ' they wait not for Rutulian
sword and fire ', i.e. to destroy their ships. **maria.** Supply
sunt as the verb and **est** in the next line.

l. 131. **rerum altera pars**, ' one half of the world ', i.e. the sea, for their ships have been lost.

l. 132. **gentes** is in apposition with **tot milia**; say ' in so many thousands, the Italian nations . . .'.

ll. 132–134. **nil . . . deorum**, ' in no way do the doom-fraught oracles of the gods make me affrighted, if the Trojans boast of (**prae se iactant**) any ', i.e. ' in no way do any of the doom-fraught oracles of the gods of which the Trojans boast . . .'.

ll. 135, 136. **sat . . . Troes**, *lit.*, ' sufficient (fulfillment) has been made to the fates and to Venus in the fact that (**quod**) the Trojans have reached . . .'.

ll. 136, 137. **sunt . . . praerepta**, *lit.*, ' there are to me too (=I have too) my destiny facing (i.e. to match theirs), to root out with the sword the accursed tribe, my wife [1] having been stolen (i.e. for the stealing of my wife) '.

l. 138. **Atridas**. The **Atridae**, *lit.*, ' sons of Atreus ', are the brothers, Agamemnon and Menelaus, the former of whom led the Greek expedition against Troy, while the latter was the husband of Helen whose abduction by the Trojan prince Paris was the cause of the war.

l. 139. **iste dolor**, ' such grief as yours '; grief i.e. at the loss of Lavinia on the part of his soldiers whom Turnus is addressing.

solisque . . . . The force of **nec** in the previous line is continued : ' and not Mycenae alone has the right to take up arms ': *lit.*, ' and not to Mycenae . . . is it allowed . . .'. **Mycenae** was the city of Agamemnon.

ll. 140–142. **periisse . . . femineum**, ' " but to have perished once is sufficient " (you say) : ay, to sin in time past (**ante**) should have been sufficient, loathing utterly hereafter well-nigh (**modo non**) all woman-kind.'

In these lines Turnus puts up an imaginary objection, only to reply that the Trojans ought to have learnt once for all from their experiences over Helen.

[1] Lavinia, daughter of Latinus. Actually she was his betrothed.

F

ll. 142–144. **quibus . . . dant.** This sentence is a strong exclamation, introduced by relative connection : it will be a help to supply an antecedent : [1] ' what men! to whom this confidence in a rampart between us (**medii**) and the delaying ditches—that separate but little from death—give courage '.

fossarum morae, *lit.,* ' the delays of the ditches ', and **leti discrimina parva,** *lit.,* ' small separations from death ', two typical Vergilian phrases. Note the genitive **leti,** a Graecism, for in Greek that case is the ' from ' case.

The argument—for Turnus' strong emotion makes him some-what incoherent—seems to be : after their experiences in the Trojan war, the Trojans ought to be women-haters and anxious above all to avoid a second abduction, especially as their refusal to come out and fight on this occasion reveals their cowardice.

ll. 144, 145. **moenia . . . manu,** ' the walls of Troy fashioned by the hand of Neptune '. The latter and Apollo built the walls round Troy for Laomedon, one of the Trojan kings and father of Priam.

ll. 148, 149. **non . . . in Teucros,** *lit.,* ' there is no need to me by the arms ', i.e. ' I need not the armour of Vulcan nor a thousand ships (to fight) against the Trojans '.

Note : (i) the construction of **opus est** with dat. and abl. (ii) the sneer at his rival Aeneas. For the armour that Vulcan made at the request of Venus for her son Aeneas, see the Introduction, p. xvii.

The thousand ships that tradition says made up the Greek expedition against Troy are famous in literature : cf. Marlowe : ' was this the face that launched a thousand ships? '

ll. 149, 150. **addant . . . socios,** ' let all the Etruscans strait-way add themselves (as) allies ', i.e. ' join in alliance '. See the Introduction, p. xviii.

[1] This edition follows the Oxford Classical Text and most editors in putting a full stop after **femineum.** Some prefer, however, to replace the full stop by a comma and allow the sentence and the sense to run straight on : ' as (men) to whom . . .'.

ll. 150–152. **tenebras . . . ne timeant**, 'let them not fear darkness . . .'. Many scholars regard l. 151 as an interpolation from II, 166, on the ground that there is no Palladium (i.e. statue of Pallas Athene) in the Trojan camp and that the words are pointless and flat. There is, however, no manuscript authority for their omission and, as Conington has shown, they reinforce the point Turnus is making, that he will not use any of the tricks and stratagems which the Greeks used at Troy.

In the Trojan war, two Greeks, Diomedes and Ulysses, had stolen from Troy the sacred image of Pallas Athene (the Palladium)—a serious blow to the Trojan morale, for they believed that the goddess's help and support depended on its safe preservation.

l. 152. **caeca in alvo. caecus** properly means 'blind', i.e. 'un-seeing'. Sometimes as here it gets the sense 'unseen', 'dark'. For the stratagem of the Wooden Horse, see, II, ll. 1–267.

l. 153. **luce**, 'in (day) -light'. **certum est**, 'it is resolved (for me)', i.e. 'I am resolved'.

ll. 154, 155. **haud sibi . . . in annum**, *lit.*, 'I will make (**faxo**) that they do not say ([**ut**] **haud ferant**) the matter is (**esse** to be supplied) for them with Greeks and Pelasgian (=Grecian) warriors whom Hector kept at bay for ten long years'.

Note : **faxo**, an old form of the future tense. Translate : 'I will make them in no way say that they are dealing with . . .'.

l. 156. **nunc adeo. adeo** is often used as an enclitic to emphasise the preceding word. **acta.** Supply **est**, 'has been spent', i.e. 'has passed'.

l. 157. **quod superest**, 'as to what is left (of the day)'.
laeti, adj. for adv., 'joyfully'. **bene gestis rebus**, abl. absol., 'things well done', i.e. 'after what you have achieved'.

l. 158. **pugnam sperate parari**, *lit.*, 'expect that battle is being prepared', i.e. 'that we are preparing for . . .'.

ll. 159, 160. **interea . . . flammis.** Note : (i) **vigilum excubiis**, *lit.*, 'with the watchings of sentries', i.e. 'with watchful sentries '. (ii) **obsidere, cingere** both depend upon **cura** and in prose would be **obsidendi, cingendi**, gen. of the gerund.

l. 161. **qui servent,** ' to guard '; subjunctive is final (purpose) introduced by the relative pronoun.

l. 162. **delecti.** Supply **sunt.** **illos quemque,** *lit.,* ' them each ', i.e. ' each of them '.

l. 163. **purpurei cristis,** ' purple with plumes '—a Vergilian variation for ' with purple-plumes '. **iuvenes,** ' warriors ', as often.

ll. 164, 165. **discurrunt . . . aenos,** ' they run to and fro (**dis-**) and take their turns, and stretched on the grass, they give free play to the wine as they tilt the bowls of bronze '. **variant vices,** ' they take their turns ', i.e. to relieve one another. ' The bowls ' are used for mixing water with wine and are tilted to fill the cups.

l. 166. **custodia,** abstract for concrete, =**custodes.**

l. 167. **ludo,** ' in revel '. There are fifty-five unfinished lines in the twelve books of the Aeneid. It seems, at times, that Vergil's flow of inspiration came to an end in the middle of a line and that such lines were left to be completed at the final revision which Vergil's untimely death prevented his carrying out. The reader will note that some of these half-lines are not only beautiful but also effective in their very incompleteness.

l. 168. **super** is an adverb, to be taken closely with **e vallo,** ' from their rampart above '.

l. 169. **alta,** the neuter pl. of the adj. is used as a noun, ' the height '. **nec non** is frequent in Vergil. **nec** =**et non,** and the two **nons** cancel one another ; **nec non,** therefore, means merely ' and '.

l. 170. **pontes . . . iungunt,** ' and join bridges and towers '. Vergil has probably in mind the defensive works of his own day in which towers were linked to the main defensive line by drawbridges.

l. 172. **si quando . . . vocarent,** ' if at any time (**quando**) adversity should call '.

l. 173. **rerum,** ' of the camp ', dependent upon **magistros. dedit,** ' appointed '. **esse.** For the infinitive after **do,** see the note on l. 362.

l. 174. **legio,** ' host '.

l. 175. **excubat exercetque vices,** *lit.,* ' keeps watch and plies the turns ', i.e. ' keeps watch in regular turn '. **quod . . . est** is explanatory of **vices,** *lit.,* ' as-to-what is to-be-defended by each ', i.e. ' each defending his post '.

l. 177. **Hyrtacides,** ' son of Hyrtacus '. These words ending in **-ides,** meaning ' son of — ', are known as patronymics. **comitem Aeneae,** ' as companion to A.' i.e. ' to accompany A.'.

Ida venatrix, ' the huntress Ida ' is the mother of Nisus.

l. 179. **iuxta** is an adverb, ' hard by '. Supply ' was ' as the verb.

quo . . . arma, *lit.,* ' than whom (abl. of comparison) was fairer no other of the followers of Aeneas nor (of those who) donned the Trojan arms ', i.e. ' fairest of all of Aeneas ' followers and of those who . . .'.

l. 181. **ora . . . iuventa,** ' a boy showing his unshaven cheeks in his first youth '—a Vergilian variation for ' a boy whose unshaven cheeks marked youth's first bloom '.

l. 182. **pariter,** ' side by side '. **ruebant.** Note the force of the imperfect : ' they used to rush '.

l. 184. **dine** is **di,** pl. of **deus** and the enclitic **-ne. addunt =** **dant.**

l. 185. **an . . . dira cupido,** ' or does his own wild desire become for each man a god? '

ll. 186, 187. **iamdudum mens agitat,** ' long has my heart been pressing (me) '. Note the tense of **agitat** with **iamdudum** and cf. the French, *depuis longtemps je vous attends,* ' I have been waiting for you a long time '. **aliquid magnum,** ' some great (deed) ', object with **pugnam** of **invadere.** The infinitive after

agitat is a poetical construction : prose would demand **ut invadam.**

l. 188. **fiducia rerum,** ' confidence in their fortunes '. **habeat,** ' possesses ', subjunctive in indirect question.

l. 189. **lumina . . . micant,** ' the watch-fires gleam (only) here and there '. It looks as if they may have been allowed to die out.

l. 190. **silent late loca,** ' the places are silent far and wide ', = ' o'er all the host reigns silence far and wide '.

l. 191. **quid dubitem,** ' what I am thinking of '. Note the meaning of **dubito,** ' I doubt ', ' hesitate '. **animo,** local abl., ' in my mind '.

ll. 192, 193. **Aenean . . . reportent.** Order for translation : **omnes, populusque patresque exposcunt Aenean acciri virosque mitti qui reportent certa.** Note : (i) **populusque.** -que means ' both ' and can be ignored. **populus, patres :** Vergil is using terms more applicable to his own day—a natural anachronism. (ii) **Aenean** has a Greek acc. ending. (iii) **qui reportent,** purpose clause. (iv) **certa,** ' sure (news) '.

l. 194. **si . . . promittunt,** ' if they promise thee what I ask '. This seems to refer to rewards that Nisus will ask for for his friend. as in the next words he disclaims all for himself but ' the glory of the deed '.

ll. 195, 196. **tumulo . . . Pallantea,** ' I seem (to myself) to be able to find (i.e. I think I can find) below yon mound a way to the walls and city of Pallanteum '.

The latter is the city of Evander, built on the site of the future Rome, where Aeneas has gone to seek aid. See the Introduction, p. xvii.

l. 197. **magno . . . amore,** ' stirred with great longing for glorious deeds (**laudum**) '. Note **laudum,** a good example of the objective genitive.

l. 199. **mene** = **me** and the interrogative enclitic **-ne.**

l. 200. **fugis** with the infinitive **adiungere** is a poetical construction, understandable, however, when **fugere** has the meaning of ' hesitate ', ' avoid ' or ' shrink from ', as it has here. **me socium summis adiungere rebus,** *lit.,* ' to join me (as) thy comrade in the highest things ', i.e. ' to let me join as thy comrade in deeds of high renown '.

l. 201. **bellis adsuetus Opheltes,** ' Opheltes accustomed to war,' i.e. ' O. experienced in battle '.

l. 202. **inter** governs **Argolicum terrorem** and **labores Troiae.** ' Argolic ' = ' Grecian '.

l. 203. **sublatum erudiit.** See the note on l. 13 and tra ¹ate ' reared and trained '. **sublatum** from **tollo.**[1]

nec . . . gessi, *lit.,* ' nor with thee did I do such things ', i.e. ' not thus, (**ita** from l. 201) with thee did I behave '.

l. 204. **fata extrema,** ' his last fate ', i.e. ' his fate to the last '.

l. 205. **hic,** = **hic meus** with **animus,** ' this soul of mine is one-that-scorns (**contemptor**) the light (of day) '.

ll. 205, 206. **et istum . . . honorem :** order for translation : **et qui credat istum honorem quo tendis bene emi vitā,** ' and one such as believes that the glory to which (**quo**) thou strivest is nobly bought with life (itself) '. **qui credat,** consecutive subjunctive.

l. 207. **Nisus.** Supply ' replies '.

l. 208. **nec fas,** ' nor (is) it right ', i.e. that I should have such fears about you.

l. 209. **referat,** present subjunctive expressing a wish for the future : ' so may great Jupiter or whosoever . . . bring back '.

ovantem, *lit.* ' triumphing ', in agreement with **me,** i.e. ' in triumph '.

l. 209. **aut . . . aequis.** There were so many gods and goddesses, major and minor, in the ancient world, each with his sphere of influence, that in prayer one had to be all-inclusive if one wanted to be quite sure that the prayer would reach the right divinity.

---

[1] **tollere** is the word formally used to describe a father's acknowledgement of his child as he lifted it up at birth.

l. 210. **si quis,** ' if any ' : then follows an interruption to the thought in a clause introduced by **quae** = **et talia,** ' and thou seest many such (dangers) in a hazard such-as-this (**tali**) ' ; then his sentence is resumed, ' if any chance or god . . .', **si quis casusve deusve . . . .**

l. 211. **in adversum,** ' into adversity '. **rapiat.** Note the mood. **me** is the object to be supplied.

l. 212. **tua . . . aetas,** ' thy years are worthier of life '.

ll. 213, 214. **sit . . . humo,** ' let there be one to rescue me from the battle or ransom me at a price and commit me to the earth '.

Note : (i) **sit,** jussive subjunctive. (ii) **qui mandet,** consecutive subjunctive, commonly found in relative clauses where the antecedent is indefinite. (iii) the translation of the perfect passive participles, **raptum, redemptum.** See the note on l. 13. The ancient world believed that those who had not had the customary burial rites were refused the passage over the river Styx which gave entry into the underworld, and so wandered a hundred years along the river banks.

l. 214. **solita . . . vetabit,** ' or if any chance, as-is-customary (**solita**) refuse (this) '. For the tense **vetabit,** see the note on ll. 99–101.

l. 215. **absenti . . . sepulcro,** ' (let there be one) to pay funeral rites to the absent and honour him with a tomb '. The latter would strictly be a cenotaph, there being no body.

l. 216. **neu sim,** ' nor let me be '. **matri miserae,** ' to thy poor mother '.

ll. 217, 218. **quae . . . Acestae.** In Book V, we learn that Aeneas having lost four ships[1] leaves in Sicily those whom it is impossible to transport further, and plans the new city of Acesta[2] for them. Apparently the mother of Euryalus was alone of the many older women not to remain in the island.

l. 220. **nec . . . cedit,** ' nor does my purpose now change or give ground '.

[1] See the Introduction, p. xv.
[2] Named after Acestes, the Sicilian king.

l. 221. **acceleremus.** Note the mood, hortative subjunctive
—' let us . . .'.

vigiles. Remember that Nisus and Euryalus are on guard
(l. 175) ; they now arouse the watch (**vigiles**) to take their place;
cf. **succedunt** (l. 222).

l. 223. **ipse comes graditur,** ' he goes (as) comrade to Nisus ',
i.e. ' he accompanies N.'.

l. 224. **cetera animalia,** ' all other living creatures '.

l. 225. **oblita,** from **obliviscor,** ' I forget ', a verb which is
followed by the genitive.

l. 226. **delecta iuventus,** ' picked warriors ', is in apposition
with **ductores . . . primi,** ' the leading captains of the Trojans '.
Teucrum is gen. pl.

l. 227. **summis regni de rebus,** ' on state matters of-high-
import ' (**summis**).

l. 228. **quid . . . esset,** indirect questions, dependent on a
verb easily supplied from the previous line : ' as-to-what
(**quid**) they should do . . .'.

Note that the direct questions would have had the delibera-
tive subjunctive, **quid faciamus,** ' what are we to do? '

l. 230. **castrorum . . . medio,** an unusual phrase—' in the
middle of the camp and of the plain '. The latter seems to have
been an open space in the middle of the camp. **una** is an
adverb.

l. 231. **admittier orant ; admittier** is an old form of the
present infinitive passive, and the use of the infinitive is
poetical.

l. 232. **rem . . . fore,** acc. and infin., depending on a verb of
saying which can easily be supplied from **orant** : ' the matter,
they said, was grave and would be well worth the delay ',
(*lit.*, ' the price of delay ').

l. 233. **accepit,** ' welcomed '. **trepidos,** ' (them) impatient ',
i.e. ' in their impatience '.

ll. 235, 236. **neve . . . ferimus,** *lit.*, ' let not this which we bring be viewed from our years ', i.e. ' let not our offer be judged by our years '.

l. 237. **insidiis,** ' for our wiles ', i.e. ' for our wily plan '.

l. 238. **qui . . . ponto,** ' which is available where the road forks by the gate nearest the sea '. **in bivio portae,** ' in-the-meeting-of-two-roads-of the gate '. The simplest way to take this expression is to assume that by the gate two roads met. Otherwise, we may follow Conington and take **bivium portae** = **porta,** for at the gate there is the way in and the way out. One road perhaps leads direct to the sea, the other turning to the left runs parallel to the shore. It is the latter that Nisus and Euryalus take to make their way through the Rutulian camp.

quae proxima. They choose the gate nearest to the sea because it is probably the least defended.

ignes, ' watch fires '.

l. 240. **erigitur,** ' rises '. The Latin passive is equivalent to the English intransitive verb. **fortuna,** abl., dependent upon **uti.** The latter would be **ut utamar** in prose.

l. 241. **quaesitum,** acc. of the supine, normally used after verbs of motion to express purpose : ' to seek '. **Aenean.** Note the Greek acc. ending again.

l. 243. **adfore.** Supply **eum** as the subject, in acc. and infin. construction after **cernetis.**

nec . . . euntes, ' the way does not deceive us as-we-go (*lit.*, going) '.

l. 244. **obscuris sub vallibus,** ' down in the dark valley ', to be taken closely with **vidimus. primam urbem,** ' the outskirts of the city ' is Conington's happy translation. Pallanteum was built on the Palatine hill.

l. 246. **hic** is an adverb. **annis gravis,** ' burdened (*lit.*, heavy) with years '. **animi,** ' in counsel ' is a genitive of respect.

l. 248. **tamen,** ' after all '.

l. 249. **tales animos iuvenum.** 'such spirits of youths':
'such spirited youths'. **certa,** 'trusty'. **cum ... tulistis,**
'seeing that you have produced ...'. Note the use of **cum**
(causal) with the indicative—a mood that is possible only when
the cause is to be emphasised as certain.

l. 251. **et vultum ... rigabat,** *lit.,* 'he watered his cheeks
and face with tears'. English idiom would prefer 'tears
poured down his cheeks ....'.

ll. 252, 253. **quae ... solvi;** order for translation: **quae
praemia, quae digna praemia reár posse solvi vobis, viri, pro
istis laudibus**'.

rear, potential subjunctive = English future, 'shall I
think'. **pro istis laudibus,** 'for such great deeds as yours'.

l. 253. **pulcherrima,** i.e. 'rewards'.

l. 254. **mores vestri,** 'your own character'.

l. 255. **pius Aeneas.** pius is the stock epithet for Aeneas
throughout the poem. It means much more than the word
'good' by which, for want of something better, it is usual to
translate it. **pius** means 'dutiful' in various relationships:
creature to creator, child to parent, citizen to community.
Aeneas is 'good' or 'dutiful' as a son, and also in his un-
questioning submission to the will of the gods.

integer aevi Ascanius, *lit.,* 'Ascanius whole in age', i.e. 'A.
youthful in years'. **aevi** is a gen. of respect, a construction
imitated by the Roman poets from Greek. Cf. **animi maturus**
in l. 246.

l. 256. **meriti ... umquam,** i.e. **non umquam immemor tanti
meriti.**

ll. 257–261. **immo ... gremiis.** In translating, follow the
order of the Latin except for **vos** which, as object of **obtestor,**
can be left until l. 260. **cui ... reducto,** 'to whom (there is)
safety alone, my sire brought back', i.e. 'whose safety alone
depends on my sire's return'. **per magnos penates.** The
'household gods' were for a Roman the tiny images kept in the
home and worshipped regularly. They were probably origin-

ally ' gods of the store '. Cf. Aeneid I, ll. 378, 379, where Aeneas says : ' I am good Aeneas, who am carrying with me in my fleet my household gods snatched from the foe '.

> **sum pius Aeneas, raptos qui ex hoste penates**
> **classe veho mecum.**

per Assarici larem ; lar is ' a household god ' and Assaracus was one of the kings of Troy. Associated naturally with the **lar** is **Vesta,** the Roman goddess of fire, in whose temple, regarded as the hearth of the nation, a fire was always kept burning. **canae,** properly ' white-haired ', means ' ancient '.

quaecumque . . **est,** is the object of **pono** in the next line and can be translated after it : ' whatever (=all) my fortunes and hopes '.

l. 262. **nihil** . . . **recepto,** ' nothing (is) sad, him recovered ', i.e. ' there is no sorrow if he is recovered '.

l. 263. **bina** =**duo,** with **pocula. argento** . . . **signis,** ' wrought in silver and rough (i.e. embossed) with figures '.

l. 264. **devicta** with **Arisba** in abl. absol. Arisba was one of several towns in the neighbourhood of Troy which, according to Homer, sent help to the besieged city and, as a consequence, may well have been sacked by the invading Greeks. But this does not explain how Aeneas, a Trojan prince, conquered it. Perhaps, as Page says in his edition, Vergil used these Homeric names to give the authentic epic flavour to his own work and so could hardly be expected to bother about avoiding inconsistencies.

l. 265. **tripodas geminos,** ' two tripods '. ' Tripods ' were of three kinds : they were tables with three legs, three-legged supports bearing a cauldron for heating water, and three-legged portable altars for sacrifice. The second sort was often given as a prize at the games.

auri . . . **talenta,** ' two great talents of gold '. How much these would be worth, it is impossible to say, and it is doubtful whether Vergil had any clear idea. The Greek talent is usually said to have been the equivalent of £233 sterling, i.e. sterling before it left the gold standard.

l. 266. **cratera,** has a Greek acc. ending. It is a Greek word imported into Latin, being the mixing bowl for the wine and water.

dat, ' is the giver ' ; idiomatic use of the present where the act itself is chiefly considered.   **quem** will then be translated by ' of which '.

Sidonia Dido. Dido was actually the daughter of the king of Tyre. ' Sidonian ' was, however, used generally for ' Phoenician ', and Tyre and Sidon were Phoenician cities.

ll. 267, 268. **si . . . sortem,** *lit.,* ' if indeed it will have fallen to me (**mihi** understood) as victor to . . .', i.e. ' if it shall be my lot . . .'. **praedae dicere sortem,** ' to assign the allotment of the spoil '.

l. 269. **equo** is the antecedent of **quo,** and **armis** of **in quibus.** They are both inside the relative clause and attracted into the case of the relative pronoun : translate as if you had **equum quo,** ' the horse on which ', **arma in quibus.**

l. 271. **excipiam sorti,** ' I shall take apart from the allotment ' : **sorti,** either dative after the compound verb, or an old form of the abl. **iam . . . praemia,** ' even now (as) thy rewards ' : **praemia** in apposition with the object acc. in the previous line.

l. 272. **genitor,** ' my father ', i.e. Aeneas. **bis sex lectissima matrum corpora,** *lit.,* ' twice six choicest persons of matrons ', i.e. ' twelve matrons of choicest person '.

l. 273. **captivos. bis sex** is understood, ' and twelve male captives, each armour to all ', i.e. ' each with his own armour '.

l. 274. **insuper . . . Latinus,** ' in addition to this, what (of) land (i.e. all the land) king Latinus himself possesses '. Note the partitive genitive.

l. 275. **te . . . insequitur.** Ascanius now addresses Euryalus, ' thee whom my age pursues at a closer interval '. Ascanius is, then, but a little younger than Euryalus.

l. 276. **venerande puer.** Ascanius has feelings of awe and veneration for Euryalus similar to those that the 1st former sometimes has for the school rugby or cricket captain.

l. 277. **comitem casus in omnes**, ' (as) my comrade for ', i.e. ' to share in all my fortunes '.

ll. 279, 280. **tibi . . . fides**, ' in thee (shall be) my greatest trust of (i.e. in) deeds and words '. Euryalus shall be his closest confidant. **contra quem**, ' in answer to him '.

ll. 281–283. **me . . . cadat**, ' me no time shall be found to prove (**arguerit**, fut. perf.) unequal to such brave (deeds of) daring ; only let fate turn out (*lit.*, fall) favourable, not un-favourable '. Note that the future perfect sometimes denotes the future situation which will result from a completed action or what will be found to have happened.

l. 283. **te**, acc. with **unum**, second acc., after **oro**—' of thee ' we say in English.

l. 285. **est mihi**, ' is to me ' = ' is mine ' *or* ' I have '. **tenuit** has two subjects, **non Ilia tellus, non moenia regis Acestae**, but agrees with the nearer. Note finally that Latin sometimes thinks of the *fact* when we think of the *possibility* : so here we prefer to say ' could keep ' for ' kept '. For ' the city of king Acestes ', see the note on l. 218.

l. 286. **excedentem**, ' as she set forth '.

l. 287. **huius . . . est**, *lit.*, ' of this, however much of peril it is ', i.e. ' this peril, such as it is '.

l. 288. **inque salutatam** = **et insalutatam**. This separation of prefix and word is known technically as tmesis, a Greek word which means ' cutting '. **testis** is the complement, ' night and thy right hand (be) witness '.

l. 289. **quod nequeam**, ' because I could not ', potential subj.

l. 290. **solare** is the imperative of the deponent **solari**.

l. 291. **sine** is the imperative of **sinere**. **tui**, ' (of) thee ', dependent upon **hanc spem**. We say, however, ' in thee '. Note the hiatus between the final vowel of **tui** and the first one of **audentior**. Normally the first would be elided. Vergil more often allows himself this licence in the third or fourth foot, especially at the caesura where there would be a natural pause in the rhythm.

l. 293. **Iulus** is the same as Ascanius.

l. 294. **patriae pietatis imago**, ' the picture of (such) love towards a parent '. **patria pietas =pietas erga patrem.** For **pietas** see the note on **pius**, l. 255.

l. 295. **tum** . . . . For the unfinished line, see the note on l. 167.

l. 296. **sponde . . . coeptis,** ' be sure that all (shall be) worthy of the great task-thou-hast-begun '.

l. 297. **mihi,** ' to me ' = 'mine '. **nomenque,** ' and only the name of Creusa shall be found to be wanting '. Note : (i) the translation of the fut. perf. **defuerit** and cf. l. 282. (ii) Creusa was the name of Iulus' mother, lost in the escape from the burning city of Troy. See the Introduction, p. xiv.

ll. 298, 299. **nec . . . manet,** ' nor slight is the honour that awaits one who bore such a son (*lit.*, such a bringing forth) '. **factum,** ' thy deed '. **quicumque casus,** nom. pl.

l. 300. **per caput hoc,** ' by this head ', i.e. his own. **solebat,** ' was wont (to swear) '.

l. 301. **reduci** is dat. in agreement with **tibi,** ' to thee on thy return '. If we take **secundis rebus,** which is also dat., closely with **reduci** as an hendiadys, we get ' on thy successful return '.

l. 302. **matrique** : the first -**que** means ' both '.

l. 304. **Lycaon** was a Cretan worker in metal. Hence **Gnosius,** for Gnosus was the name of the chief town in the island.

l. 305. **habilem,** *lit.,* ' for holding ', i.e. ' for wearing '.

l. 307. **exuvias.** Take this in apposition with **pellem** by ignoring the -**que** after **horrentis,** ' the skin stripped off a shaggy lion '. **permutat,** i.e. by taking Nisus' helmet.

l. 308. **quos euntes,** ' them on their way '.

l. 309. **iuvenumque senumque.** Translate this phrase immediately after **primorum,** ' of the chieftains ', with which it is in apposition. The first -**que,** ' both ', can be ignored.

l. 310. **nec non.** See l. 169.

l. 311. **ante annos,** ' beyond his years '.   **gerens,** ' displaying '.

l. 312. **portanda,** ' to-be-carried ', gerundive.

l. 315. **multis . . . exitio,** ' destined, however, to be first the death of many '.   Note : (i) the word **tamen** shows that some of the thought is suppressed : i.e. ' (though going to their own death), yet they would first inflict many losses on the foe '. (ii) **exitio** is a dat. of purpose with second dat. **multis.**

l. 316. **somno vinoque,** ' in drunken sleep ', a good example of what is known as an hendiadys—i.e. the putting of two nouns in the same case, linked by ' and ', when logically one should depend upon the other in the gen. case or be an adjective, as here.   Cf. **paterae et aurum,** ' bowls of gold ' or ' golden bowls '.

l. 317. **fusa** is from **fundo,** ' I pour ', and suggests the abandon of drunken sleep, ' outstretched '.   **arrectos . . . currus,** ' chariots on end on the shore '.

l. 318. **iacere,** from iaceo (2).

l. 319. **vina,** ' wine (-goblets) '.

l. 320. **audendum dextra (est),** *lit.,* ' it is to-be-dared with a right hand ' ;   ' deeds of daring need the (strong) right arm '.

l. 321. **hac,** ' by this (path) ', i.e. ' here '.   **ne qua manus,** *lit.,* ' that-not any hand ', =' that no hand '.

l. 322. **a tergo,** ' from behind '.   **consule longe,** ' watch far ' (=' over a wide field ').

l. 323. **haec . . . dabo.   vasta dabo,** forms the same notion as **vastabo.**

ll. 325, 326. **qui . . . somnum,** ' who, it chanced (**forte**), raised up on a lofty coverlet, was breathing forth slumber from all his breast '.   The heavy breathing of drunken sleep is well described.

l. 327. **rex . . . augur,** ' a prince too (**idem**) and of prince Turnus an augur most beloved '.   An augur was one who foretold the future from the interpretation of various signs, e.g. the flight of birds, the behaviour of certain sacred animals, or the condition of animals' entrails.

l. 328. **pestem,** ' the plague (of death) '.

l. 329. **iuxta,** adv., ' hard by '.   **temere . . . iacentes,** ' just as they lay amid their arms '.   It might be helpful to keep to the order of the Latin, translating this line first, although it is the object of **premit,** ' he overwhelms '.

l. 331. **nactus,** ' getting (him) '.   **nactus** from **nanciscor.**

l. 332. **ipsi domino.**   Latin often uses the dative where we prefer the genitive.

l. 333. **sanguine singultantem,** *lit.,* ' sobbing with blood ', an expressive phrase for ' spurting blood '.

l. 335. **illa** is abl. with **nocte.**   **plurima,** acc. pl. neut., adverbial acc. with **luserat.**   Supply **premit** in ll. 334-5.

ll. 336, 337. **multoque . . . victus,** ' and lay, his limbs overcome in deep sleep '.   **membra** is acc. of respect with **victus,** *lit.,* ' overcome as to his limbs '.   **multo deo** is taken to refer to the god of sleep : others refer the phrase to the god of wine.

ll. 337, 338. **felix . . . tulisset,** ' happy he, had he without-pause (**protinus**) made that game as long as (*lit.,* equal to) the night and continued it until dawn '.

l. 339. **impastus . . . .**   Begin the simile with **ceu.**

l. 340. **manditque.**   The -**que** ' both ' may again be ignored.

l. 341. **mutumque.**   The -**que,** linking the two adjectives **molle** and **mutum** is unnecessary in English.

l. 342. **nec . . . caedes,** ' nor less (is) the slaughter of Euryalus '.

l. 343. **in medio,** ' in his path '.   **sine nomine,** ' nameless ', is used with **plebem** as an adjective.   This attributive use of prepositional phrases becomes common in the time of Vergil and Livy.

l. 344. **subit,** ' falls upon ' ;   an unusual meaning.

l. 345. **ignaros . . . videntem,** ' (these) unconscious (all) ; yet (he fell upon) Rhoetus . . .'.

G

l. 346. **magnum** agrees with **cratera,** the latter having the Greek acc. ending.

ll. 347, 348. **pectore . . . condidit,** 'full in his breast (**in adverso pectore**) as he rose (*lit.,* to whom rising) to-meet-him (**comminus**) he buried his sword to-the-hilt (**totum**) '.

l. 348. **et multa . . . purpureum,** 'and drew it back crimson with the flowing blood ' ; *lit.,* ' with abundant death '.
The text follows the Oxford Classical Text in putting a semicolon after **purpureum** in l. 349 and reading the masculine form for **purpuream** which is found in all manuscripts except one. If the latter reading is adopted, line 348 ends with a full stop and **purpuream** agrees with **animam** : the translation will then be ' he drew it back steeped in death. Rhoetus belches forth his blood-red life . . .'.

l. 350. **vina,** pl. for sing. **hic . . . instat,** ' he (i.e. Euryalus) hotly presses on his-stealthy-course (**furto**) '. The latter is dative after **instat.**

l. 351. **ibi . . . .** Begin with **videbat,** then the two acc. and infinitives. **ignem** (probably sg. for pl.) **. . . extremum,** ' the watch-fires were almost out '.

l. 353. **talia** is object of **ait,** l. 355.

l. 354. **sensit.** Supply **eum** as the subject of **ferri.**
nimia caede atque cupidine, probably an hendiadys, ' by excessive lust for slaughter '. See the note on l. 316.

l. 355. **lux inimica,** ' the dawn that-is-our-foe '.

l. 356. **poenarum . . . est,** *lit.,* ' sufficient of vengeance has been drained by us ', i.e. ' we have had our fill of vengeance '.

l. 357. **multa . . . .** **multa** agrees with **arma,** (the **-que** may be ignored) but in sense can be taken with **virum** (genitive pl.), ' the arms of many heroes '.

l. 359. **et aurea bullis cingula,** ' and his gold studded sword belt ' ; object with **phaleras** of **rapit,** l. 364.

ll. 360–362. **Tiburti . . . Caedicus.** Order for translation : **dona quae olim ditissimus Caedicus mittit Remulo Tiburti cum**

iungeret (eum, i.e. **Remulum) hospitio absens** ('though-he-was-far-away').

Note : (i) **ditissimus = dives.** (ii) **mittit,** idiomatic use of the present for the past. See the note on l. 266.

l. 362. **ille,** i.e. **Remulus. dat[1] habere,** ' gave (them) to keep '. Note this poetical use of the infinitive to indicate the purpose of an action—a construction which is very frequent in Greek and therefore so familiar to Vergil and other Roman poets that perhaps unconsciously they introduced it into Latin along with other fashions of speech more characteristic of Greek than their own tongue.

Finally note that grammarians believe that the infinitive of both languages was originally the dative case of a verbal noun, so that **habere** is properly ' for keeping '.

l. 363. **post mortem,** i.e. of Remulus. This is a difficult line unless we can assume that the Rutulians got possession of the belt by attacking and defeating the grandson. The line is regarded as spurious by some scholars.

l. 364. **nequiquam** may be taken either with **fortibus** or with **aptat.**

l. 366. **tuta capessunt,** ' make for safety '. **tuta,** acc. pl. of the neuter adj. used as a noun. We have had other examples.

l. 367. **praemissi,** ' that had been sent forward '. **ex urbe Latina,** i. e. Laurentum.

l. 368. **cetera legio,** ' the rest of the host '. **campis = in campis.**

l. 369. **responsa ferebant.** We are not told what request had been made by Turnus of the Latins at Laurentum, but probably it was for reinforcements. Hence the ' thrice hundred (**ter centum**) led by Volcens '. **Volcente magistro,** *lit.,* ' Volcens (being) master '.

l. 372. **cum . . . cernunt,** ' when they saw '. **cernunt** is historic present and the indicative is used after **cum** because it is an ' inverse ' **cum** clause, i.e. the **cum** clause really contains

---

[1] Historic present.

the main verb but the status of main to subordinate clauses is
' inverted ' for the sake of effect. **hos . . . limite,** ' them
turning off by the path to-the-left '. As long as Nisus and
Euryalus are making their way through the lines of Turnus'
camp, they follow a route parallel to the coast. Then they turn
to their left in order to pass the end of the Stagno di Levanto
and make a straight course for the City of Evander where
Aeneas is. A position near Castel Fusano probably marks the
spot, for it is here that we are told by modern travellers that
the Silva Laurentina begins and covers the whole of the area
with impenetrable thickets. This position is suitable whether
we place Laurentum north of the Numicus river or south of it.
See Gaston Boissier, *The country of Horace and Vergil*, pp. 284
sqq. and Bertha Tilley, *Vergil's Latium* (passim).

l. 373. **sublustri . . . umbra,** ' in night's glimmering shadow '.

l. 374. **radiisque . . . refulsit,** *lit.,* 'and facing the rays (of the
moon) flashed back ', i.e. ' and caught and reflected the moon-
light '.

l. 375. **haud . . . visum,** *lit.,* ' not heedlessly was it seen '.
As we shall see, Volcens took immediate action.

l. 377. **nihil illi tendere contra,** ' they made no reply '.

tendere is an historic infinitive—the first example we have
had so far—i.e. the infinitive is used as the equivalent of a
perfect indicative : **tendere = tetenderunt.** The sentence could
also be taken to mean ' made no movement in reply '.

l. 378. **celerare, fidere** are historic infinitives.

l. 379. **ad divortia nota,** ' at the well-known forks '.

l. 380. **hinc atque hinc,** ' here and there '. **custode,** sing. for
pl., ' with guards '.

ll. 381, 382. **silva . . . horrida,** *lit.,* ' the forest was bristling far
and wide with thickets and dark ilex ' ; i.e. ' the extensive
forest was dense with . . .'.

l. 383. **rara . . .,** ' here and there shone the path among the
dim (*lit.,* hidden) tracks '.

l. 384. **tenebrae ramorum.** ‘ darkness of the branches ’, seems to be the opposite of an hendiadys, i.e. =‘ darkness and branches ’.

l. 385. **fallitque . . . viarum,** ‘ and fear deceives him in the direction of the paths ’, i.e. ‘ fear makes him lose his way ’.

l. 386. **imprudens,** ‘ heedless(ly) ’, i.e. not knowing that he had lost Euryalus.

l. 387. **atque locos . . .,** ‘ and (got to) the place which was afterwards called Alban from the name of Alba (at that time (**tum**) king Latinus kept there his lofty stalls) ’.

l. 389. **ut,** ‘ when ’.

l. 391. **sequar,** probably future indic., rather than present subj. (deliberative).

ll. 391, 392. **rursus . . . silvae,** ‘ again retracing (*lit.*, un-rolling) all the confusing path of the deceptive forest ’.

ll. 392, 393. **simul . . . legit,** ‘ at the same time also he watches for and picks his steps backward ’. For **observata legit,** see the note on l. 13.

l. 394. **strepitus,** acc. pl. **signa sequentum,** ‘ the calls of the pursuers ’.

l. 395. **nec . . . tempus,** *lit.*, ‘ nor long time is in the middle’, i.e. ‘ and no long time elapses ’.

ll. 396–398. **quem . . . frustra.** Order for translation : **quem iam oppressum fraude loci et noctis, subito tumultu turbante, omnis manus rapit, et conantem plurima frustra.**

Note : (i) **fraude . . . noctis,** *lit.*, ‘ by the deceit of the ground and of the night ’, i.e. ‘ by the ground and dark that had deceived him ’. (ii) **subito . . . turbante,** *lit.*, ‘ a sudden onset confusing (him) ’, would be better in the passive : ‘ confused by a sudden onset ’. (iii) **et conantem . . . frustra,** *lit.*, ‘ though trying (i.e. though he-resisted) strongly (but) in vain ’. **plurima,** adverbial acc.

l. 399. **quid faciat,** ‘ what is he to do? ’, deliberative sub-junctive (see the note on ll. 67, 68). So also **audeat, inferat, properet.**

l. 400. **moriturus,** *lit.*, ' about to die ', i.e. ' to his death '.

l. 402. **ocius,** though comparative in form, means just ' quickly '. **adducto lacerto,** ' his arms pulled to (his chest) '. Translate : ' quickly pulling his arms to his chest, aiming his spear and . . .'. Note that ' and ' has to be supplied before **suspiciens.**

l. 404. **praesens** is to be taken closely with **succurre,** *lit.*, ' at hand do thou assist ', i.e. ' be thou at hand to assist '.

l. 405. **Latonia custos.** The moon-goddess is identified with the huntress-goddess Diana, who was the daughter of Latona : hence **Latonia,** ' Latona's daughter '. **decus** and **custos** are in apposition.

l. 406. **qua,** ' any ' with **dona.**

l. 407. **ni . . . auxi,** ' if I myself have increased (i.e. worshipped) (thee) in any way by my hunting '. **qua** is acc. pl. neut., adverbial acc. with **auxi** which is used here in its religious meaning of ' honour ', ' worship '.

l. 408. **tholo : sacra ad fastigia. tholus** is the dome inside the temple and **fastigia** the pediment outside. The latter, which is the triangular space formed by the gabled roof, was usually filled with sculptured figures.

l. 409. **sine,** imperative of **sinere.**

l. 410. **toto . . . corpore,** *lit.*, ' having striven with his whole body ', i.e. ' with the full force of his body '.

l. 412. **venit . . . Sulmonis,** *lit.*, ' comes into the back of Sulmo, turned away ', i.e. ' hits Sulmo full in the back '.

l. 413. **frangitur,** ' breaks '. The Latin passive equals the English intransitive use.

l. 414. **volvitur,** ' rolls '. See the previous note. **flumen,** i.e. of blood.

l. 415. **frigidus.** Note : (i) the weight and emphasis that falls on the adjective in its position as first word in the line, especially when followed by a pause in the sense. (ii) the effective contrast between **calidum (flumen)** and **frigidus.**

English, being non-inflected, has to use periphrasis to get a similar effect, although Milton copied this idiom effectively in *Paradise Lost*. Translate by, ' now cold in death '.

longis . . . pulsat, *lit.*, ' beats his sides in long sobs ', i.e. ' his sides heave in . . .'.

l. 416. **diversi**, ' this way and that '.

ll. 416, 417. **hoc . . . ab aure**, ' all the more fiercely (*lit.*, by this the fiercer) again (*lit.*, the same man) behold! he poised another missile from the tip of his ear '.

l. 418. **Tago . . . utrumque**, ' through both temples of Tagus'. Note the dative where we prefer the genitive.

l. 419. **traiectoque . . . cerebro**, ' and stuck-fast, warmed in his pierced brain '.

l. 420. **conspicit**, ' cannot glimpse '. See note on l. 285.

l. 421. **teli auctorem**, ' the one who shot the dart '. **nec quo . . . possit**, indirect question dependent upon **conspicit**, ' nor where he can hurl himself in-his-rage (**ardens**) '.

l. 422. **tu . . . .** Volcens is addressing Euryalus.

l. 424. **ibat**, ' he began to move ', the inceptive use of the imperfect.

l. 425. **celare** depends upon **potuit** in the next line.

l. 426. **amplius**, ' any longer '.

ll. 427, 428. **me, me . . .** Note how effectively Vergil conveys the deep emotion and agitation of Nisus by the staccato phrases and ungrammatical structure of the sentence. In his agony, Nisus blurts out ' me, me, here I am, I did it, on me turn your sword . . .'.

l. 428. **nihil . . . potuit**, ' naught he; he neither did the deed nor could (have) '. **nihil nec** do not cancel out.

l. 429. **caelum . . . testor**. **conscia** probably goes with both nouns: ' yon (**hoc**) sky and the stars, that-know-the-truth (**conscia**) I call to witness '.

l. 430. **tantum**, ' only '.

l. 431. **viribus . . . adactus,** ' the sword driven with force '.

l. 434. **conlapsa,** ' drooping ' ; the deponent perfect participle, as often, having the force of the English present.

l. 435–437. **purpureus . . . gravantur.** This lovely and pathetic simile is borrowed from Homer, *Iliad* VIII, 306–8. Catullus (XI, 22), also has : **velut prati ultimi flos praetereunte postquam tactus aratro est** : ' just as when a flower on the edge of the meadow has been touched by the passing ploughshare '.

Begin with **veluti cum purpureus flos. lassove . . . collo,** ' or poppies with drooping neck '. **demisere = demiserunt. cum,** ' when '. **pluvia,** ' by a shower '.

l. 438. **in medios,** ' into the midst (of the foe) '.

l. 439. **petit,** ' makes for '. **in solo . . . moratur,** ' to Volcens alone gives all his attention '.

l. 440. **quem circum = circum eum** (i.e. Nisum). **hinc atque hinc,** ' from here and from there ', i.e. ' from all sides '.

l. 441. **non setius,** *lit.,* ' not otherwise ', i.e. ' just as fiercely '.

l. 442. **Rutuli clamantis in ore adverso,** ' full in the face of the shrieking Rutulian '. For the translation of **adverso,** see l. 412. **et moriens . . .,** ' and himself dying, robbed his enemy of life ', *lit.,* ' took life from his enemy '.

l. 443. **condidit.** Supply ' it ' as the object.

l. 445. **placida in morte,** ' in the calm of death '.

l. 446. **si . . . possunt,** ' if my poems have any power '. **quid,** adverbial acc. with **possunt.**

l. 447. **memori aevo,** *lit.,* ' from mindful time ' = ' from the memory of time '. For the translation, cf. l. 445.

l. 448. **dum . . . accolet,** 'as long as the house of Aeneas shall dwell on the Capitol's unmoved rock '. The house of Aeneas is the Roman people. The **Capitolium** is the southern peak of the hill called **Mons Capitolinus.** On it stood in Vergil's time the great temple dedicated to **Jupiter Optimus Maximus, Juno** and **Minerva.** It meant very much to the Romans what Westminster Abbey means to us.

l. 449. **pater Romanus**, ' the father of Rome '—a phrase in which Vergil and his readers would recognise a tribute not only to the emperor Augustus but also to every ' Roman father '. For amongst the Romans, there was a deep emotional attachment to the home and to the ' head of the household ', ' the Roman father', and in this reverence for the home, for mother and father, perhaps lay the source of their strength and stability, and their willingness to accept discipline and sacrifice.

These two lines which mean merely : ' while Rome shall last ', are an excellent example of the power of poetry to express this and all the national and emotional associations of such a sentiment.

These noble lines form a fitting epilogue to the moving story of Nisus and Euryalus—a story which reveals at its best Vergil's power of appealing to our human feelings.

l. 450. **Rutuli = Latini**, ' the Latins ', for they came from Laurentum. But Vergil loosely uses the name of their allies ' the Rutulians ' instead. **potiti**, from **potior**, a verb which governs the abl. case.

ll. 452–454. **nec . . . Numaque**, ' just as heavy (*lit.*, nor less) in the camp was the sorrow when Rhamnes was found lifeless and so many chieftains had been done away in one murderous-attack (**caede**), (like) Serranus and Numa '. The name **Numa** creates a difficulty because Vergil does not mention him amongst the victims of Nisus. Two solutions have been suggested : (i) either read **Lausoque** here or **Numamque** in l. 334. One scholar[1] has gone so far as to say that he is convinced Vergil would have done one or the other, if he had revised the poem.

l. 454. **ingens concursus**, ' (there was) a mighty rush ', i.e. ' they rushed in large numbers '.

l. 456. **plenos . . . rivos** ; we say ' (to) the full streams *of* foaming blood '.

l. 457. **inter se**, ' among themselves ', i.e., ' in talk with each other '.

---

[1] Ribbeck.

ll. 459, 460. **et iam . . . cubile.** Note this poetical way of saying ' it is dawn '. These two lines occur in Book IV, 584, 585.

Aurora is the goddess of the dawn and Tithonus is her husband. **prima,** adj. for adv., ' first '. **novo lumine,** ' with fresh light '.

l. 461. **iam . . . retectis,** two abl. absols. : *lit.,* ' now the sun having been poured in and now things unveiled in light ', i.e. ' now that the sun was pouring in and unveiling all nature with his light '.

l. 462. **Turnus . . . ipse.** Begin with **Turnus ipse circumdatus armis.**

l. 464. **quisque,** ' each (leader) '.

l. 465. **quin,** ' nay more '. **visu miserabile,** ' a piteous sight ', *lit.,* ' piteous in-the-seeing '. The ablative of the supine in -u is used only, as here, to limit the meaning of an adjective (abl. of respect).

l. 467. **Euryali et Nisi.** For the unfinished line, see the note on l. 167.

l. 468. **duri,** ' much-enduring ', ' hardy '.

l. 469. **opposuere** = opposuerunt. **cingitur,** ' is bounded '.

ll. 471, 472. **simul . . . tabo** ; Note : (i) **virum,** gen. pl. ' of the (two) warriors '. (ii) **nota nimis miseris,** *lit.,* ' known only-too-well to them grieving ', ' that they their grief knew only too well '. (iii) **movebant** has as understood object ' them '. (iv) use ' but now ' for -**que** after **atro** to obtain a suitable contrast.

l. 473. **pavidam** goes with **urbem.**

l. 474. **nuntia,** ' (as) messenger '. In Book IV, ll. 174–190, Vergil describes Rumour as a winged monster ' who beneath every feather in her body, strange to tell, has a watchful eye, speaking tongue and lips, and a straining ear '.

l. 475. **at . . . reliquit.** Translate as if you had : **subito misera calor ossa reliquit** : **misera ossa,** ' her wretched frame '.

l. 476. **excussi . . . pensa,** ' from her hands dropped (*lit.*, was knocked) the shuttle and her work was unwound'. **radii, pensa,** pl. for sg. The latter was strictly the amount of wool allotted for a day's spinning.

l. 477. **femineo ululatu.** There is an hiatus between these two words, i.e. the **o** of the former word is not slurred before the **u** of the latter. See also l. 291.

l. 478. **scissa comam,** ' tearing her hair'. **comam** is the true direct object of **scissa** which has an active meaning, ' having torn '. The explanation is that in Greek there exists a third voice of the verb, the middle, which, as its name suggests, partakes of the nature of both active and passive, for it has very much the same *forms* of the latter but the *meanings* of the former, with the additional notion that the act is done reflexively, *to* or *for* the doer. This Greek use, imitated by Vergil and other Roman poets, is known as the middle use of the passive voice. **amens,** ' madly '. **cursu petit,** *lit.*, ' in a run makes for ' =' runs to '.

ll. 479, 480. **non . . . memor.** **illa,** not required grammatically, is effective in its pathos, ' not mindful she of men, not she of peril from the darts '. Note : (i) **virum,** gen. pl. Ancient custom forbade women to mix indiscriminately with men. (ii) **pericli telorumque** is taken as an hendiadys. See the note on l. 316. (iii) **dehinc** is scanned as a monosyllable.

l. 480. **hunc . . .,** ' is it thus that I behold thee, Euryalus? Couldst thou, the one (**ille**) (that wast to be) the final solace of my old age . . .'.

ll. 483, 484. **nec . . . matri,** ' and was not the chance (**copia**) given (**data est**) to thy poor mother to speak to thee for-the-last-time (**extremum**) when thou wast sent on such a dangerous task? '

l. 485. **terra ignota,** local abl., ' in an . . .'. **data**[1] **praeda,** nom., in apposition with the unexpressed subject of **iaces,** ' as prey to-be-given '.

---

[1] **data** is the reading of the MSS. and the O.C.T. Some editors prefer the correction **date,** i.e. the voc. of the perf. part. pass., ' o thou that hast been given as prey '.

ll. 486, 487. **nec te . . . produxi. tua funera** is a difficult expression. Amongst several explanations, none of which is completely satisfactory, perhaps the simplest and best is to take **tua funera** in apposition with **te**—a pathetic correction, as the Loeb edition says—and the phrase as meaning, with pl. for sing., ' thy corpse ' : hence we get, ' nor thee—thy corpse —did I, thy mother, lead forth (to burial) '.

l. 487. **pressive,** ' nor did I close '.

l. 488. **festina** is an adverb.

l. 489. **tela** is 1st declension fem., ' a loom '.

l. 490. **quo sequar,** deliberative subj., ' where am I to follow '. **quae** goes with **tellus** as the subject : ' what land '.

l. 491. **funus lacerum,** ' thy mangled corpse '. **hoc . . . refers,** ' is *this* (all that) thou bringest back to me from (=of) thee, my son '.

l. 492. **hoc . . .,** ' (is) *this* (what) I followed . . .'.

l. 493. **si qua est pietas,** ' if there is any pity (to you), i.e. ' if you have any pity '.

l. 495. **miserere,** imperative, 2nd sing., of the deponent **misereor. tuo** goes with **telo** in the next line, ' with thy weapon' i.e. ' thunderbolt '.

l. 496. **sub Tartara,** ' down to Tartarus '. Tartarus, 2, m., or Tartara, 2, n.pl., are commonly used in Latin for the underworld, the abode of the dead ; occasionally in a more restricted meaning, as that part of the underworld in which the wicked live.

invisum hoc caput, ' this accursed head ' ; **caput** is often used poetically for ' person ', ' creature '. Euryalus' mother is referring to herself.

l. 497. **quando,** ' since '.

l. 498. **concussi** : supply **sunt.**

ll. 500–502. **illam . . . reponunt.** Begin : **Idaeus et Actor monitu Ilionei et multum . . . Iuli corripiunt illam incendentem luctus** (acc. pl.)—**que reponunt.**

interque . . . reponunt, ' among their hands (i.e. taking her in their arms) place her safely (**re** =in **reponunt**)[1] inside ' (**sub tecta**).

l. 503. **terribilem sonitum** is a kind of cognate acc. with **increpuit,** ' rang out its dread sound '. Note that in two different ways, accusatives may depend upon *in*transitive verbs : (i) to run *a race*, true cognate acc. because ' race ' is cognate, or related in meaning to ' run '. (ii) to run *two miles*, adverbial acc. of *extent of action*. **terribilem sonitum** is akin to (i).

l. 505. **Volsci** = **Itali,** ' Italians ', one tribe being used for the race as a whole. **acta . . . testudine,** ' their roof of shields driven on in even line ', i.e. ' driving on . . .'.

In his description of the attack on and defence of the Trojan camp, Vergil is using expressions and techniques more suitable to his own day, all of which would be very familiar to his countrymen, many of whom had at one time or another served in the Roman armies during the period of the Civil Wars. For example, ' the roof of shields ', or ' tortoise-shell formation' was used in storming walled towns or fortified camps. The men of the front rank closed in, held their shields in front ; the men on the flanks held theirs on the sides, while the others raised theirs over their heads, overlapping one with the other and forming a sloping angle like a roof. This formation gave almost complete protection against all but the heaviest missiles. When they had thus reached the enemies' defences, their job was to fill and cross the ditch, and begin to breach the palisade or wall. Cf. l. 506.

l. 507. **pars,** ' some '. **quaerunt,** agreeing in number with the logical, not grammatical subject, has two objects : **aditum,** ' a way in ' and the infinitive **ascendere,** ' to climb '. The latter use is poetical.

ll. 508, 509. **qua . . . viris,** ' where the line is thin and the ring of defenders (**viris**) shows gaps (*lit.*, shows light) (being) not so close '. **viris** is really an abl. of respect with **spissa.**

---

[1] *lit.,* ' duly '.

l. 509. **effundere, detrudere** are historic infinitives. **telorum** depends upon **omne genus.**

l. 511. **adsueti,** nom. pl. masc. in agreement with **Teucri,** ' well trained by a lengthy war '. The war, of course, is their ten years' defence of their city.

l. 512. **infesto pondere,** abl. of description with **saxa,** ' stones of deadly weight '. **si qua,** ' (to see) if anywhere '. **qua** is the adverb that corresponds to the indefinite pronoun **quis.**

l. 513. **tectam aciem,** ' the armoured rank ', i.e. the tortoise-shell formation. **cum tamen,** ' all the while, however '. **cum** is purely temporal here.

l. 514. **iuvat,** ' it delights (them) '. Note this meaning of **iuvare** when it is used impersonally. The idea seems to be that the attackers beneath their close-packed shields experience a feeling of exhilaration as missiles of every sort fall harmlessly upon their protective armour.

omnes casus, acc. pl., ' all that befalls ' is a translation that reminds us that **casus** is derived from **cado,** ' I fall ', and has, therefore, its literal meaning here as well as its common connotation of ' chance ', ' accident '. **densa,** ' closely-packed ' *or* ' compact '.

l. 515. **nec . . . sufficiunt,** ' and now they do not suffice (= have not the strength) (to break through) '. **qua,** ' where '.

l. 516. **ruunt,** ' throw down '.

l. 517. **armorum tegmina,** ' the protection of their armour ', = ' their protecting armour '.

l. 518. **nec amplius,** ' no longer '. **curant** with the infinitive is poetical. **caeco Marte,** ' in blind warfare ', ' in battle in-the-dark ', i.e. under the shield of the tortoise-shell formation.

l. 519. **vallo,** ' from the rampart '.

l. 520. **certant** with the infinitive is poetical. In prose only a few verbs like **volo, nolo, malo, conor, audeo,** etc. have the dependent infinitive, called prolative, which ' carries on ' the sense. The poets, however, treated many other verbs in the same way. We have had three examples in the last ten lines. For the unfinished line, see the note on l. 167.

l. 521. **parte alia,** ' in another part (of the field) '. **horrendus visu,** ' dreadful in the seeing ', i.e. ' to behold '. For the ablative of the supine, see the note on l. 465. **Mezentius** l. 522 is the subject.

l. 522. **pinum Etruscam** (l. 521), ' his Etruscan pine (torch) '. Mezentius is king of Etruria, that district that lies immediately north of the line of the Tiber ; an impious and cruel man, he is described by Vergil as **contemptor deum,** ' one who scorned the gods '. (VIII, 7).

l. 523. **equum = equorum.** The taming of the horse caused a great revolution in remote antiquity and the warriors that achieved it and used the horse (originally to draw chariots) became a ruling aristocracy in the settled lands around the Mediterranean.

l. 525. **Calliope** was the chief of the nine Muses. The poet addresses them all, but mentions only one by name. **aspirate canenti,** *lit.,* ' breathe upon (me) singing '. As the indirect questions in the next two lines are dependent upon **canenti,** we may say : ' inspire my song as I tell '.

For the invocation, a common feature in the epic tradition, see the note on l. 78.

ll. 526, 527. **quas . . .,** order for translation : **quas strages quae funera Turnus ediderit ferro tum ibi et quem virum** (what hero) **quisque demiserit Orco.**

tum, ' then ' = ' in that battle '. **Orco,** poetic dat. of the place whither = **ad Orcum** of prose. Orcus was one of the names of the god or king of the underworld and also of the underworld itself. Hence, ' to send down to Orcus ' is a poetical variant for ' to slay '.

l. 528. **et . . . belli,** ' and unroll with me the mighty scroll (*lit.*, border) of the war '. Vergil's metaphor is that of a scroll which had to be unrolled by the reader.

l. 529. **et . . . .** This line, the same as Book VII, 645, is omitted by the better MSS. and is, therefore, suspect and believed to have been inserted from the earlier book.

ll. 530, 531. **turris . . . loco quam,** ' there was a tower of vast height and lofty gangways, suitably placed, which . . .'. Note : (i) **turris.** See the note on l. 505. The tower is a defensive structure, made of wood and connected by gangways to the walls of the camp. (ii) **vasto . . . altis,** two abls. of description. (iii) **opportuna loco,** *lit.,* ' suitable in its position ', **loco** being an abl. of respect.

l. 532. **omnes Itali,** i.e. the Italian tribes led by Turnus, chieftain of the Rutuli, who is organising the attack on the Trojan camp while Aeneas, the Trojan leader, is on a visit to Evander.

expugnare, evertere depend upon **certabant,** ' strove to storm, to overthrow '. This use would not be permissible in prose, but the poets found the present infinitive active such a convenient form metrically that they used it frequently after a large group of verbs, in addition to the regular use after the so-called modal ones. See the note on l. 520. **summa opum vi,** *lit.,* ' with the utmost force of their resources '.

l. 533. **Troes contra,** ' (while) the Trojans on-the-other-hand (**contra**) (strove) '. **certabant** has to be supplied and the infinitives **defendere** and **intorquere** are dependent upon it.

l. 534. **densi** is grammatically in agreement with **Troes** but is best translated with **tela intorquere** as an adverb ' to hurl darts in showers '.

l. 535. **lampada** has the acc. ending of the Greek 3rd declension.

l. 536. **lateri,** ' in the side (of the tower) '. **quae plurima vento,** *lit.,* ' which very much with the wind ' = ' fanned by the wind '.

l. 537. **tabulas,** ' planks '. **et postibus . . . adesis** = **postibus haesit et adedit (eas),** ' clung to the doors and consumed (them)'. For the translation, see the note on l. 13.

H

l. 538. **trepidare, velle** are historic infinitives, i.e. they are to be translated as **trepidaverunt, voluerunt.** The latter ='wished for', i.e. ' sought '. **malorum fugam,** ' escape from disaster '; **malorum,** objective genitive. The relation of **malorum** to **fugam** is similar to that between a direct object and its verb.

l. 540. **in . . . caret,** ' to (that) side which is free from harm '. **pondere subito,** ' with the sudden weight ', =' suddenly overweighted '.

l. 541. **procubuit, tonat.** For the change of tense, see the note on l. 35. **omne** agrees with **caelum.**

ll. 542–544. **semineces .... Begin : semineces veniunt ad terram** and keep fairly closely to the order of the Latin.

Note : (i) **immani . . . secuta,** *lit.,* ' the huge mass having followed (them) ', abl. absol. Turn, however, into the passive, ' followed by . . .'. (ii) **pectora . . . ligno,** ' their breasts impaled by the cruel splinters ', *lit.,* ' impaled as-to-their breasts ', **pectora** being an acc. of respect.

l. 545. **elapsi,** i.e. **elapsi sunt.**

l. 546. **serva Licymnia,** ' Licymnia (a) slave '. **Maeonio regi,** ' to *or* for the Maeonian king '. ' Maeonian ' means ' Lydian ', Lydia being a district in Asia Minor. **furtim,** ' secretly ', because her child.was illegitimate.

l. 547. **sustulerat,** from **tollo. vetitis armis,** ' in forbidden arms ' : perhaps because his royal father had forbidden him.

l. 548. **ense . . . alba,** ' light-armed with naked sword and white shield, without fame **(inglorius)** '. The latter adjective refers to his shield which bore no device, for he was as yet too young to have proved himself.

l. 549. **isque ubi,** i.e. -**que ubi is,** ' and when he '.

l. 550. **hinc . . . Latinas,** acc. and infin., ' on this side and on that the Latin lines standing '.

l. 551. **ut fera,** ' like a wild-beast '. **venantum,** ' of hunters ', gen. pl. of **venans,** strictly the present participle of **venor.** It depends upon **densa corona.**

l. 552. **seseque** . . . **inicit,** ' and hurls itself on death, not unknowing (=wittingly) '.

l. 553. **et** . . . **fertur,** *lit.,* ' and with a bound is carried (=rushes) down upon the spears '.

l. 554. **haud aliter,** *lit.,* ' not otherwise ', =' even so '. **moriturus,** *lit.,* ' about to die ', i.e. ' to certain death '.

l. 555. **et qua** . . . **tendit,** i.e. **et tendit qua** (where) **videt tela densissima.**

l. 556. **pedibus** . . . **Lycus,** ' far better in his feet ', i.e. ' far swifter-footed '. **inter et hostes.** et means ' both ' and can be ignored.

l. 557. **tenet,** ' reaches '. **certat,** ' strives '. See the note above on l. 532. **alta tecta,** ' the top of the wall '.

l. 558. **socium** =**sociorum.** See the note on ll. 6, 7.

l. 559. **quem** =**eum.** It is unnatural in English to use the relative pronoun after a major stop. This idiom is known as relative connection and is best turned by personal or demonstrative pronouns.

quem pariter . . . **secutus,** ' pursuing him alike on foot and with his spear '. Note the translation of the perfect participle of the deponent verb, how it often has the meaning of the English *present* participle.

l. 560. **his,** i.e. **verbis. victor,** ' victorious ', ' in his hour of victory '.

ll. 560, 561. **nostrasne** . . . **manus ;** order for translation : **sperastine te posse evadere nostras manus, demens?**

l. 562. **pendentem,** ' hanging ', i.e. ' as he hung '. **revellit.** Supply ' him ' as the object.

l. 563. **qualis ubi,** ' even as when '. The full construction is (**talis**) **qualis,** ' such as '.

ll. 563–566. **qualis ubi** . . . **lupus.** Begin **qualis ubi Iovis armiger petens alta sustulit uncis pedibus** . . . .

Note : (i) **Iovis armiger,** i.e. the eagle which was believed to carry Jove's thunderbolts. (ii) **petens alta,** *lit.,* ' seeking high (things) ', **alta** is acc. pl. neut. : i.e. ' soaring aloft '. (iii) **candenti corpore** is abl. of description with **cycnum**, ' of (snow)-white body '.

l. 565. **quaesitum . . . .** Order for translation : **aut (qualis ubi** to be supplied) **lupus Martius rapuit a stabulis agnum quaesitum matri multis balatibus.**
Note : (i) **quaesitum**, perf. part. pass., with **matri**, dat. of the agent where prose would have **a matre** ; *lit.,* ' sought by its mother '. (ii) **lupus Martius**, ' the wolf of Mars ', ' of Mars ' because Romulus and Remus, his sons, were suckled by a she-wolf.

ll. 569–576. **Ilioneus . . . Capys.** In these lines we have an account of the casualties on both sides : the sentence actually consists of a string of nominatives and accusatives (subject-object) with *one* common verb, **sternit,** ' lays low '. The catalogue is interrupted occasionally by descriptive or participial phrases.

ll. 569–570. **Ilioneus . . . ferentem :** order for translation : **Ilioneus** (sternit l. 571) **Lucetium saxo atque . . . montis subeuntem** (as-he-draws-near) **portae et ferentem ignes** (fire-brands). **saxo . . . montis,** ' with a stone, a huge fragment of a mountain '.

l. 571. **Emathiona,** Greek acc. ending.

l. 572. **hic . . . hic,** i.e. Liger . . . Asilas. **longe . . . sagitta,** *lit.,* ' the arrow deceiving afar off ', is usually translated : ' with the arrow that stealeth from afar '.

l. 573. **Caenea,** Greek acc.

l. 575. **pro,** ' in front of '. **Idan,** acc. **summis pro turribus,** either ' in front of the towers above ', i.e. Idas was on the wall : or ' on the topmost towers '.

l. 576. **levis,** adj. for adv., ' lightly '.

ll. 576–580. **hunc . . . rupit. hunc** refers unusually to Privernus. **ille** also refers to him. **proiecto . . . demens,** ' flinging down his shield, the fool '. **adlapsa (est) alis,** i.e. ' glided on wings ', i.e. ' sped on its winged way '. **et . . . manus,** ' and to his left side his hand was pinned '.

The change of subject is awkward, **sagitta**, the subject of **adlapsa**, being also the subject of **abdita** and **rupit**. The awkwardness can be overcome if we turn the sentence round, ' and . . . pinned his hand '. **abditaque intus**, ' and burying itself deep '. **spiramenta animae**, *lit.*, ' the breathing-holes of life ', i.e. the lungs. Translate : ' where a man draws his life's breath '.

l. 582. **pictus** . . . **Hibera**, ' with embroidered cloak, and shining in Iberian purple '. **pingere acu,** *lit.*, ' to paint with the needle ' is regular for ' to embroider '. **chlamydem** is regarded as the accusative object, used after the perfect participle passive used in a middle sense, *lit.*, ' having (embroidered his cloak) '. See the note on l. 478. Iberian means Spanish.

l. 584. **eductum** . . . **flumina**, ' reared (in agreement with **quem**) in the grove of Mars near the stream of Symaethus '. **Arcens** is a Sicilian and **Symaethus** is a river on the east coast of Sicily. The name of the son is not known.

Some MSS. and most editions read **matris**, i.e. ' reared in his mother's grove ' and assume that she was some nymph who lived near the river Symaethus.

l. 585. **pinguis** . . . **Palici**, ' where there is an altar of Palicus rich and readily appeased (=kind) '. The altar receives many costly offerings and so the god is readily appeased. The Palici were two Sicilian deities, sons of Jupiter, and said to be worshipped particularly near the river Symaethus which flows near Mt. Etna. There seems to be no particular reason, except perhaps a metrical one, why Vergil speaks of only *one* Palicus here.

ll. 586, 587. **stridentem** . . . **habena.** Order for translation : positis (=depositis, ' laying aside ') hastis **Mezentius ipse adducta habena** (' with tightened thong ') **ter egit** (=whirled) **circum caput stridentem fundam.**

l. 588. **liquefacto plumbo**, ' with molten lead '. It was generally believed in the ancient world that the heat generated by movement was sufficiently strong to melt a leaden bullet in its passage through the air. **adversi,** *lit.,* ' of (him) facing ', **i.e.** ' as he faced him '.

l. 589. **multa harena,** abl., ' over much sand ', i.e. ' over a great stretch of sand '.

ll. 590–592. **tum primum** . . . . Begin : **tum primum bello Ascanius ante solitus terrere fugaces feras dicitur intendisse** . . . .

Note : (i) **Ascanius dicitur,** ' Ascanius is said ' : we prefer the impersonal ' it is said that Ascanius '. (ii) **bello,** ' in war ' as opposed to hunting. (iii) **ante** is an adverb.

l. 593. **cui** . . . **erat,** ' to whom (=whose) surname was Remulus '. Note the interesting idiom by which **Remulo** agrees in case not with **cognomen** as you would expect but with **cui** (dative).

l. 594. **nuper thalamo sociatus,** ' lately united in marriage '.

l. 595. **is,** i.e. **Numanus. digna** . . . **relatu,** *lit.,* ' (things) meet and unmeet in the uttering,' i.e. ' words meet and unmeet to utter '. Vergil is referring not to bad language but to boasts that were unmeet in regard to his position and experience as a warrior.

l. 596. **tumidusque** . . . **regno,** ' and swelling as-to-his-heart' (acc. of respect) ; i.e. ' his heart swollen with his new royalty '. He had just married a princess, Turnus' younger sister.

l. 597. **et ingentem** . . . **ferebat,** ' and bore himself huge (i.e. and he swaggered) with a shout (i.e. shouting) '.

l. 598. **non =nonne.** With **pudet** supply **vos,** ' are you not ashamed? '

l. 599. **bis capti Phryges.** The first occasion was when Hercules sacked Troy because he had been cheated by Laomedon, the father of Priam ; the second was when the city was destroyed by the Greeks.

Phryges, ' Phrygians ', properly natives of Phrygia, a country of Asia Minor in which lay Troy, is often used by Vergil and other Roman poets for ' Trojans '. **et** . . . **muros,** *lit.,* ' and to set walls in front of death ', i.e. ' as a fence against death '.

l. 600. **en qui,** ' lo! (these are they) who . . .'. **nostra conubia,** abstract for concrete = ' our wives '. In a natural exaggeration, Numanus accuses the Trojans of wanting to rob them of their wives : actually Aeneas was a suitor for the hand of the unwed Lavinia, daughter of Latinus.

l. 601. **Italiam** = **ad Italiam.**

l. 602. **Atridae.** See the note on l. 138. **nec . . . Ulixes,** ' nor Ulysses, (that) fashioner of tales ' (*lit.*, ' of telling '). **fandi** is the gen. of the gerund of **for** (1 dep.), a very common verb in Vergil. **Ulysses** (in Greek Odysseus) is the hero of Homer's second great epic, the **Odyssey.** His Homeric epithet is (Odysseus) ' the man of many wiles ', a well-deserved tribute to his courage, resourcefulness and presence of mind which enabled him to overcome many difficulties in his ten year voyage from Troy to his home on the island of Ithaca. When he appears four hundred years later in the plays of the Athenian dramatists, we find that it is his low cunning and knavery that are emphasised. When we remember that it was Ulysses who was responsible for the trick of the ' Wooden Horse ' [1] we can perhaps understand the sneer in this line. Cf. Turnus' speech, ll. 154 sqq., in which we get a similar taunt : viz. the Trojans have now to deal with more active foes who are superior warriors to the proud and crafty Greeks (as represented by the Atridae and Ulysses). This theme is elaborated in the next few lines, and his vaunting speech ends in his vigorously stressing the contrast made by the effeminate Trojans.

l. 603. **durum . . . genus,** *lit.*, ' a hardy race from the stock ', in apposition with the subject of **deferimus** : i.e. ' a race of hardy stock '. **primum.** There are four stages in this ' tough ' training.

l. 604. **saevo gelu et undis,** ' with the water's savage cold '. For the hendiadys, see the note on l. 316.

l. 605. **pueri**—the second stage. **venatu** (dat.) . . . **fatigant,** ' (as) boys they devote themselves to (*lit.*, are awake over) hunting and give the forests no peace (*lit.*, weary them) '.

[1]See the Introduction, p. xiv.

l. 606. **ludus (est)**, ' their sport is '.   **spicula tendere arcu,**
' to shoot arrows from the bow '.

l. 607. **iuventus**—the third stage, *lit.*, ' manhood ', i.e. ' as
men '.   **patiens operum,** ' enduring hardships ', **operum** being
an objective gen., commonly found with participles.   **parvoque
adsueta,** ' and accustomed to little '.

l. 608. **rastris,** ' with heavy hoes '.   They were used chiefly
for breaking up heavy lumps of earth.

ll. 609, 610. **omne . . . hasta,** ' every age is spent in using the
steel and we goad the backs of our bullocks with the butt of the
spear (*lit.*, the spear turned) '.   The sentiment is clear : our
hands are toughened with the spear which we use either against
our enemies or as a goad for our cattle and a hoe to tame the
earth.
The final syllable of **fatigamus,** though naturally short, is
lengthened by ictus or the stress.

l. 610. **senectus**—the fourth stage.

l. 612. **canitiem . . . premimus,** *lit.*, ' we press our grey hairs
with the helmet ', a Vergilian variation for ' the helmet still
presses our grey hairs '.

l. 613. **iuvat,** ' it pleases (us) ', i.e. ' it is our delight '.
vivere rapto, ' to live on what we have plundered '.

ll. 614, 615. **vobis . . . cordi (est)**, ' your garments (are)
embroidered with saffron and gleaming purple, to you (**vobis**
understood) sloth (is) a delight ', i.e. ' you delight in . . .'.

l. 615. **iuvat,** again ' it pleases (you) '.

l. 616. **et . . . mitrae,** ' and your tunics have sleeves, and
your caps (have) strings '.

l. 617. **o vere Phrygiae . . . Phryges,** ' O Phrygian women, for
Phrygian men you are not! '   The Phrygian race lived in that
corner of Asia Minor nearest to Europe where stood the city of
Troy.   Although the Roman people were traditionally de-
scendants of Trojan settlers, Vergil puts into the mouth of
Numanus all the Roman contempt for the Oriental, his dress

and his effeminate luxury. The Romans regarded dancing as a sign of intoxication or of insanity. They also despised those who wore tunics with sleeves or the Eastern headgear, a kind of bonnet with ' ribbons ' or ' strings ' which passed over the hair and fastened at the nape of the neck or under the chin.

l. 618. **Dindyma,** is a mountain in Asia Minor, sacred to Cybele, ' the Idaean Mother '. **ubi . . . cantum,** ' where the pipe gives forth its double strain to the accustomed (worshippers) '. **biforem,** in agreement with **cantum,** might go better with **tibia,** for the ancients played on two pipes at once.

l. 619. **tympana . . . .** In the worship of the Mother goddess Cybele, music on the timbrel, pipe and flute played an important part in exciting the frenzy of her devotees. For the ' Mother ' and the significance of the adjective ' Berecyntian ', see the notes on l. 82.

l. 620. **sinite . . . ferro,** ' leave arms to men and quit the sword, (*lit.,* withdraw from) '. Just as l. 617, **o vere Phrygiae . . .,** is the climax of the first taunts, so here the emphasis falls on **viris,** ' men ', a word tacitly contrasted with the worshippers of Cybele, many of whom in their religious frenzy emasculated themselves in honour of the goddess.

ll. 621, 622. **talia . . . Ascanius,** ' (him) boasting such things and uttering ill-omened (words) Ascanius could not brook ', i.e. ' such boastful and ill-omened words Ascanius . . .'. For the translation of **tulit,** see the note on l. 285.

l. 622. **obversus,** ' turning towards (him) '. **nervo equino,** abl. of instrument with **intendit,** ' he aims his arrow with the horse-hair string '.

l. 623. **diversaque . . . ducens,** ' and drawing his arms apart '. **diversa** is a good example of the proleptic use of an adj. Cf. ' she scrubbed the floor clean ' and note how the adj. expresses the *result* of the verb's action, a use which is called ' proleptic '.

l. 624. **ante,** adv., ' first '.

l. 627. **aurata fronte,** abl. of description with **iuvencum.** It was customary to gild the horns of animals offered in sacrifice.

l. 628. **pariterque . . . ferentem,** ' and carrying his head in the same way with (=as high as) his mother '.

l. 629. **iam . . . harenam,** ' such as can already attack with his horn and scatter the sand with his hoofs '. Note **qui =talem ut is** ' of such a kind that he ' with consecutive subjunctives.

l. 631. **intonuit laevum,** ' thundered on the left '—a good omen according to Roman interpretation, especially when the sky was or seemed cloudless.

The Romans may seem superstitious in the way they interpreted what we regard as natural phenomena. Thunder in particular was regarded with great awe : cf. Horace *Odes* III, 5, i : **caelo tonantem credidimus Iovem regnare,** ' we have (always) believed from his thundering, that Jupiter was lord in heaven '. In another passage, *Odes* I, 34, ll. 2 sqq., Horace heard thunder in a sky without clouds—an experience which caused him to reject the mechanistic views associated with the Epicureans and to believe in the supernatural. Cf. **caeli de parte serena** of the previous line. **laevum** is an adverbial acc.

l. 632. **horrendum** is an adverbial acc. with **stridens. adducta,** ' drawn to (him) '.

l. 636. **tantum,** ' only '. Supply ' spoke ' as the verb.

l. 638. **aetheria plaga,** local abl., ' in the expanse of heaven '. **crinitus,** ' long-haired '. Apollo in ancient art is shown with unshorn locks—as a sign of his eternal youth.

l. 641. **macte . . . ad astra,** ' a blessing on thy young valour, my child : in this way men reach the stars '. **macte** is properly the voc. of **mactus,** ' honoured ' ; with or without **esto,** it is used as an exclamation of applause or congratulation : ' bravo! ', ' well done! ' ' Reaching the stars ' means achieving immortality. **itur** is a good example of an intransitive verb used impersonally in the passive.

l. 642. **dis . . . deos,** ' O (thou) son of (*lit.*, sprung from) gods and destined-to-be-the-sire (*lit.*, to produce) gods '. The latter are Julius Caesar and Augustus, members of the Julian clan which claimed Iulus (Ascanius) as the founder of their line.

ll. 642, 643. **iure . . . resident,** ' rightly all wars destined-to-come by fate shall sink to rest beneath the house of Assaracus '. The latter being fifth of the Trojan kings, the last phrase means ' beneath the house of Troy ' and refers now to the descendants of it, viz. the Romans. Finally, the sentence emphasises two facts : (i) **fato ventura :** war had been the destiny, not the choice, of Rome. (ii) the closing of the temple of Janus by Augustus in 29 B.C.—a sign that throughout the Roman Empire there was peace.

l. 644.. **nec . . . capit,** ' nor can Troy hold thee ', i.e. ' Troy is not wide enough for thee '. Vergil proudly refers to the great expansion of Roman power over the Mediterranean world. **simul . . . effatus** = simulac (' as soon as ') **haec effatus est.**

l. 646. **formam vertitur oris,** ' he changes the appearance of his face '. **formam,** direct object acc. after a passive verb used in a middle sense. See the note on l. 478.

The assumption of mortal shape is another epic convention, commonly used by Homer, Vergil and other authors.

l. 647. **antiquum in Buten,** ' into (that of) old Butes '. **Dardanio Anchisae.** The scansion of the line should be noted. The last syllable of **Dardanio** is not elided before **Anchisae** and the fifth foot is a spondee.

l. 648. **ante** is an adverb. **fidusque . . . custos,** ' and a faithful watcher at his gate '.

l. 649. **tum . . . addidit,** ' then his father (i.e. Aeneas) had assigned (him, i.e., Butes) (as) companion to Ascanius', i.e., after the death of Anchises.

l. 650. **omnia,** ' in all things ', adverbial acc. with **similis** and elaborated later in the similar accusatives **vocem, colorem,** etc. **coloremque.** The -que is elided before the et of the next line. Such an elided syllable at the end of a line is known as hypermetric.

l. 651. **et saeva . . . arma,** ' and in arms savage in sounds ', **sonoribus** being an abl. of respect. Translate : ' and in savage-sounding arms '.

l. 653. **sit . .,** ' let it be sufficient, son of Aeneas, that . . .'.

l. 655. **paribus armis,** dat., dependent upon **invidet,** 'arms rivalling (his own) '. Apollo was supreme in archery.

l. 656. **cetera . . . bello,** ' in other matters (=otherwise) my child, refrain from war '. **'bello** is dative. **cetera,** adverbial acc.

l. 657. **mortales aspectus** =aspectus (pl. for sg.) **mortalium,** ' the sight of men '.

l. 660. **pharetramque . . . sonantem,** ' and heard his quiver rattle in-his-flight (=as he fled) '.

l. 661. **dictis . . . Phoebi,** ' at the word and will of Phoebus '. **avidum pugnae,** ' eager (though-he-was) for the battle '. **pugnae,** objective genitive.

l. 663. **in aperta pericula,** ' into the jaws of danger ' is Conington's translation. **mittunt,** ' fling '.

l. 664. **totis . . . muris,** ' all along the walls over the battlements '.

l. 665. **amenta,** ' thongs '. Attached to javelins, probably to the middle, they gave the thrower additional power and force.

l. 667. **dant sonitum flictu,** ' give forth a sound (=resound) in the clashing (=as they clash) '.

ll. 668–671. **quantus . . . rumpit.** Note : (i) **quantus** (with **tanta** understood) ' as great as '. Continue, ' the storm that coming from the West . . .'. (ii) **pluvialibus Haedis,** ' when the Kids bring-the-rain ', abl. of ' time when '. The constellation ' the Kids ' rises in September-October, a time of stormy and rainy weather, which it was naturally believed to cause. (iii) **quam multa grandine** =tanta quanta grandine,[1] ' as thick as the hail with which '. (iv) **horridus austris,** ' wild with southern gales '. The two things compared are the storm of missiles and the storm of rain or hail.

[1] The full construction is : **tanta quanta grando est qua,** ' as great as is the hail with which '. **grando** is attracted into the relative clause and the case of the correlative **quanta.**

l. 672. **creti**, perf. part. pass. of **cresco**, ' grown from ', i.e. ' sprung from '.

l. 673. **silvestris**, ' the wood nymph '. **Iovis luco**, ' in the . . .'.

l. 674. **abietibus** is scanned as four syllables, the i being regarded as the consonant j ; **ābjĕtĭbūs**. **iuvenes aequos** is acc., in apposition with **quos**, ' youths equal to (=as tall as) . . .'.

l. 675. **quae . . . commissa (erat)**, ' which by their leader's command had been entrusted (to them) '.

l. 676. **freti . . . hostem**, ' relying on their weapons and actually invite the foe into the walls '. **armis** is emphatic ; they are relying for defence not on their walls but on their weapons.

    moenibus =**in moenia**. For **ultro**, see the note on ll. 6, 7.

l. 677. **dextra . . . pro turribus**, ' on the right and the left in front of the towers '. The men were just inside the gate and were guarding either the tower over this gate or the fortifications generally.

    There are two other ways of taking this phrase : (i) ' like towers '. (ii) ' in place of towers ', i.e. the two heroes were a ' tower of defence '.

l. 678. **et . . . corusci**, *lit.*, ' and gleaming as to their lofty heads with plumes ', **alta capita**, acc. of respect. Translate : ' with gleaming plumes on their . . .'.

ll. 679–682. **quales . . . capita** : order for translation : (tales) **quales** (even as) **geminae quercus consurgunt aeriae circum liquentia flumina sive ripis** (' on the banks ') **Padi seu propter amoenum Athesim -que attollunt intonsa capita caelo.**

    Note : (i) **caelo** = **ad caelum** in prose. (ii) **sublimi . . . nutant**, *lit.*, ' nod with their crowns on high ', becomes in English ' nod their crowns . . .'. (iii) the simile is based on Vergil's own boyhood memories in the Lombardy plain. Owing nothing to Homer and the late epic poets, it has a spontaneous charm which is often lacking in the more elaborate and artificial similes.

    The Athesis is a river in Venetia, now the Adige.

l. 683. **inrumpunt . . . patentes.** aditus is acc. pl. with
patentes in agreement. **ut videre** = ut viderunt, ' when . .'.

l. 685. **praeceps animi,** ' impetuous in temper '. animi is the
locative case.

l. 686. **totis agminibus,** ' with all their columns ', i.e. that
they were leading . . . . **versi terga dedere** = versi sunt et terga
dederunt. Note that when a subject has two verbs, it is usual
to express the first of the two actions by a perfect participle
passive, here in agreement with the subject.

l. 687. **posuere,** ' laid down '.

l. 688. **tum . . . irae,** ' then angry passions (irae) increase the
more in their opposing hearts '.

l. 689. **collecti glomerantur** = collecti sunt et glomerantur.
See the note above. **eodem,** ' at the same spot '.

l. 691, 692. **ductori . . . hostem fervere,** ' to Turnus, the
chieftain raging (i.e. as he rages) in a different part (of the
battle) and dismays his enemies (**turbanti viros**), news is brought
that the foe is flushed . . .'.

l. 693. **caede nova,** ' with blood newly-shed '.

l. 696. **Antiphaten** has a Greek acc. ending. He is a bastard
son (**nothum**) of noble Sarpedon (**Sarpedonis alti**). The latter
was an ally of the Trojans, and came from Lycia in Asia Minor.
Thebana, ' Theban ' refers, therefore, not to the famous Thebes
in Greece but to ' Thebe ', a town in Mysia, also in Asia Minor.
Hence **Thebana de matre,** ' from a mother from Thebe '. **is enim
. . . agebat,** ' for he first impelled himself (towards Turnus) ',
i.e. ' was advancing '.

l. 699. **sub altum pectus abit,** ' makes its way deep into the
breast '.

l. 700. **reddit . . . spumantem,** ' the cavity of the dark
wound ', (i.e. the dark gaping wound) 'gives back a foaming
flood '.

l. 702. **Erymanta** is the acc. of **Erymas**.

l. 703. **Bitian** is the acc. of **Bitias**. Supply **sternit** as the
verb from the preceding line.

l. 704. **non iaculo,** ' not with a javelin '. **dedisset,** ' he would have given up '.

l. 705. **magnum stridens,** ' hissing mightily ', i.e. ' with a mighty hiss '. **magnum** is adverbial acc.

The **phalarica** was strictly not a weapon of epic times. It was chiefly used in the third century B.C. by the people of Saguntum (in Spain), had a heavy head of iron and a ball of lead at the other end. Propulsion was normally by means of the catapult. Here Turnus hurls it by hand.

l. 706. **fulminis acta modo,** *lit.,* ' driven in the manner of a thunderbolt ', i.e. ' driven like a thunderbolt '.

l. 707. **duplici squama et auro,** ' with double scales of gold '— a hendiadys for which see the note on l. 316.

l. 708. **conlapsa ruunt,** ' give way and fall '. See the note on l. 686.

l. 709. **dat genitum,** ' give forth a groan '. **clipeum** is here neuter in the nom. with **ingens** in agreement. **super,** adverb, ' on top (of him) '.

ll. 710–716. **talis . . . Typhoeo.** This long, elaborate and very artificial simile is rendered all the more difficult by literary allusions which may have taxed the understanding even of the educated reader in Vergil's day.

l. 710. **talis . . . quondam,** ' so on the Euboean shore of Baiae at times '. Baiae is near Cumae, which, situated on a promontory in the bay of Naples, possesses ' Euboean shores', because the original settlers in this Greek colony had come from the island of Euboea, off the coast of Attica in Greece.

l. 711. **saxea pila,** ' a mass of stone '. Vergil is referring to the common practice of building for wealthy Romans villas on piers that jutted out into the sea. Cf. Horace, *Odes* III, 1, ll. 33 sqq., **iactis in altum molibus.**

ll. 711, 712. **magnis . . . iaciunt,** ' which first framed of huge blocks they hurl into the sea '. **ponto** is dative, a case often used in poetry for *place whither.* Prose would demand a preposition with its case.

ll. 712, 713. **sic . . . recumbit**, ' so it, falling forward (**prona**) drops with a crash (**ruinam trahit**) and, dashing into the waters (**inlisa vadis**) sinks deep (to the bottom) '.

l. 714. **miscent se**, ' are in turmoil '. **nigrae harenae.** It has been pointed out by commentators that the adjective is used correctly here because the sand of the bay of Baiae is formed out of lava.

l. 715. **Prochyta alta.** Prochyta is a small island off the Campanian coast opposite Baiae. Its modern name is Procida. **tremit** has two subjects, **Prochyta** and **Inarime. durum cubile** is in apposition with **Inarime** in the next line.

l. 716. **Inarime . . . Typhoeo**, ' Inarime by Jove's command, piled upon Typhoeus '. **Inarime**, ' a rugged couch ' (**durum cubile**) is a name coined by Vergil either deliberately or in misunderstanding from a passage in Homer.[1] At any rate, he has linked with the Homeric story an Italian island (now Ischia) of which the real name was Pithecusa (in the bay of Naples).

Typhoeus is variously described as a hurricane or as a fire-breathing giant or as a monster with a hundred heads. He was subdued by Jupiter with a thunderbolt and buried under Aetna or, as here, the island of Pithecusa. The eruptions of Aetna and other volcanoes were thus supposed to be caused by such fire-breathing monsters as Typhoeus as they lay crushed beneath the mountain's weight.

l. 719. **Teucris**, dat., ' among the Trojans '.

l. 720. **conveniunt.** The understood subject is 'the Latins '. **quoniam . . . pugnae**, ' since the opportunity of fighting has been given (them) '.

l. 721. **animo incidit**, ' has fallen upon their hearts ', i.e. ' has taken full possession of them '.

l. 722. **ut**, ' when '. **fuso corpore**, ' vanquished body ' is an abl. of description with **germanum.** It might be translated as : **germani fusum corpus.**

[1] *Iliad*, ii, 783.

l. 723. **et . . . res,** indirect questions, dependent upon **cernit,** ' and in what position their fortune is (=how stands the battle) and what chance controls the fighting (**res**) '.

l. 725. **obnixus . . . umeris,** ' pushing with his broad shoulders '.

l. 727. **ruentes,** ' (them) rushing ', i.e. ' as they rush '.

ll. 728, 729. **demens qui . . . viderit . . . incluserit,** ' madman in that he did not see . . . and actually shut (him) in . . .'. **qui** + subj. is often used with various adverbial meanings such as purpose (very common), consequence, concession and cause. The **qui** clause here gives the *cause* of his being called **demens.**

Note : (i) **Rutulum regem,** ' the Rutulian prince ', i.e. Turnus. (ii) **in medio agmine,** ' amidst the throng '. (iii) **ultro.** See the note on ll. 6, 7.

l. 730. **immanem . . . tigrim,** i.e. **veluti immanem tigrim inter . . .**

l. 731. **oculis,** ' from his (i.e. Turnus ') eyes '.

l. 732. **horrendum,** adv. acc., ' dreadfully '.

l. 734. **clipeoque . . . mittit,** ' and from his shield he hurls flashing lightnings ', i.e. ' flashes of lightning '. The subject is Turnus.

l. 735. **turbati,** *lit.,* ' confused ', ' dismayed ', i.e. ' in confusion *or* dismay '.

l. 736. **mortis . . . ira,** ' blazing with anger *at* his brother's death '. **mortis** is a kind of objective genitive.

ll. 737, 738. **non haec . . . Turnum.** The emphasis falls on **haec** : ' this (is) not Amata's bridal palace, (this is not) the middle of Ardea (that) holds Turnus within his native walls '.

Amata, wife of Latinus and mother of Lavinia, favoured Turnus as her daughter's suitor. The bridal palace is, therefore, Laurentum. Ardea is the chief city of the tribe of Turnus, the Rutulians.

l. 739. **nulla hinc exire potestas,** ' no chance to escape from here (is to thee) ', i.e. ' thou hast no chance . . .'. The infinitive

E

exire depends upon the verbal notion implicit in **potestas.** Prose would have **exeundi.**

l. 740. **olli** = **illi,** dat. sg. This is an obsolete form, revived by Vergil to dignify his work with touches of the antique. This slow-moving line, with its maximum proportion of spondees, emphasises the quiet confidence of Turnus.

l. 741. **si qua . . . virtus,** ' if (there is) any courage in thy heart ', i.e. ' if thy heart has any courage '.

l. 742. **inventum (esse),** perf. infin. pass. ' Thou shalt report to Priam that here too an Achilles has been found '. Priam, king of Troy, was slain in the capture of Troy. ' Thou shalt report to Priam ' = ' thou shalt go to the underworld to report '.

l. 743, 744. **ille . . . hastam :** order for translation—**ille adnixus summis viribus intorquet hastam rudem nodis et crudo cortice. ille** is Pandarus.

l. 745. **excepere aurae,** ' the breezes received it ', i.e. the spear missed its mark. **vulnus veniens,** ' the coming wound (i.e. blow) '.

ll. 747, 748. **at . . .** Turnus is speaking. **neque . . . auctor,** ' for not such (is) the author of the weapon or the blow ', i.e. ' he who aims the weapon or the blow '. **is** is condensed for **talis ut effugias,** ' of such a kind that thou escape '.

l. 749. **et sublatum . . . ensem,** ' and rises on to his high uplifted sword '. **sublatum.** Look up **tollo.**

l. 750. **mediam** is proleptic with **frontem dividit,** ' he cleaves his brow in twain '.

l. 753. **arma . . . cerebro,** *lit.*, ' his armour bloody with brain ', i.e. ' his armour stained with bloody brains '.

l. 754. **sternit,** ' he lets fall '. **illi** is strictly the dat. of **ille,** ' to him ' : when taken with **caput,** it means ' his head '. Its emphatic position and demonstrative nature may best be rendered in English, however, by ' see! ' **partibus aequis,** ' in equal halves '.

l. 757, 758. **et si continuo . . . subisset, ultimus ille dies fuisset,** ' and if straitway such care had entered into (= had seized) the victor to . . ., that day would have been the last '.

l. 758. **rumpere, immittere.** The infinitives depend upon the verbal notion implied in **cura.** Prose would have the genitive of the gerund. Note the character of Turnus as delineated by Vergil : he is bold and fearless, but wild and almost barbarous, a warrior who neglects, in his lust for carnage, to take full advantage of the opportunities offered to him by the fortune of war. In comparison with him, Aeneas seems restrained and civilised.

l. 761. **egit in adversos.** For the unfinished line, see the note on l. 167.

l. 762. **succiso poplite,** abl. absol., ' his ham[1] having been cut through ', i.e. ' ham-stringing him '.

l. 763. **excipit,** ' he catches '. **hinc . . . hastas,** *lit.,* ' he hurls the spears having been taken hence, at (them) fleeing '. ' hence ' = ' from them ', i.e. Phaleris and Gyges. **raptas ingerit hastas.** See the note on l. 13 and translate : ' he seizes the spears and hurls them . . .'.

fugientibus in terga can be taken closely together . ' at the backs of those who flee '.

l. 765. **addit Halyn comitem,** *lit.,* ' he adds Halys (as) their comrade ', ' to join (them) ', i.e. his dead companions.

l. 766. **ignaros . . . cientes,** ' then, all unawares on the walls and rousing the battle '. As they were facing the enemy *outside* the camp, they did not see Turnus' approach.

l. 767. **Noemonaque.** . The -que is scanned long, being influenced by its position before the two following consonants.

l. 768. **Lyncea . . . vocantem,** ' Lynceus making for him (i.e. Turnus) and calling on his comrades '. This line is the object of **occupat,** l. 770. The order of the Latin should, however, be retained.

[1] i.e. ' the back of the knee '.

l. 769. **vibranti** . . . **dexter**, *lit:*, ' having-made-a-mighty-effort with flashing sword from the rampart on-the-right ', i.e. ' with a tremendous and powerful blow of his flashing sword . . .'. **occupat**, *lit.*, ' he forestalled ', i.e. ' he smote first '.

l. 770. **huic**, means ' his ' and goes with **caput**. The adverb **comminus** is used attributively[1] with **uno ictu**, ' by one close-dealt blow '.

l. 772. **vastatorem Amycum**, object, as are the accusatives in l. 774, of **occupat**, to be supplied from l. 770. **quo . . . alter ungere . . . armare**, ' than whom no other (was) more skilled to anoint . . . and to arm '.

Note : (i) **quo**, abl. of comparison. (ii) **ungere, armare**. This poetical use of the infinitive to limit an adjective is sometimes called expexegetic, i.e. giving further explanation. Although imitated from Greek, this use is quite natural for the infinitive is in origin the dative of a verbal noun.

l. 774. **Crethea**, Greek acc. ending. Note the pathetic repetition of Cretheus' name.

ll. 775, 776. **cui . . . nervis**. There are three subjects, **carmina, citharae** (pl. for sg.) and the infinitive **intendere** ; the verb is **erant** (to be supplied) and **cordi** is the complement, *lit.*, ' to whom songs . . . are a delight ', i.e. ' who delights in . . .'. **numeros intendere nervis**, *lit.*, ' to stretch notes upon the strings ', a Vergilian variation for ' to stretch the strings with notes ', i.e. ' to play notes upon the stretched strings '.

l. 777. **canebat**, ' he sang of '.

l. 780. **receptum**, ' received ', i.e. inside the camp. Translate merely by ' within '.

l. 781. **quo . . tenditis**. **tendere fugam** is ' to direct one's flight ', and **deinde** = ' next '.

l. 782. **moenia**, ' stronghold '.

l. 783. **o cives**. The use of ' citizens ' is quite effective here. Mnestheus wishes to remind them that they are a ' citizen army ', fighting for all that is near and dear to them.

---

[1] i.e. like an adjective.

l. 785. ediderit, miserit. The future-perfect is commonly used in indignant questions with ' shall ' meaning. ' Shall one man . . . have caused . . . have sent . . . ? ' **Orco=ad Orcum** of prose. See the note on l. 527.

ll. 786, 787. non . . . pudetque. non = nonne, ' have you no pity, cowards, no shame for your unhappy country . . .'. Note the use of **pudet. pudet sceleris me**, means ' I am ashamed of my crime '. Here there is no suggestion that the Trojans should be ashamed of their country : rather Mnestheus feels that the thought of their country should arouse *their* shame at *their* cowardice.

l. 788. talibus, ' by such (words) '.

l. 789. excedere, historic infinitive, i.e. it is equivalent to **excedit.**[1] This use is most effective in the narration of a rapid succession of events as in this passage. So **petere, incumbere, glomerare.**

l. 791. hoc, abl. of cause, ' because of this '.

l. 792. ceu . . . Begin with **ceu cum,** ' as when '.

l. 794. acerba tuens, ' glaring angrily '. Note **acerba,** neut. pl. acc., used adverbially.

ll. 794–796. et neque terga . . . virosque, ' and anger or courage allows (him) for all his eagerness, neither to turn tail nor can he push on against (his foe) through spears and hunters ' **(viris).**

ille quidem hoc cupiens, *lit.*, ' he desiring this '. **ille** not required grammatically has with **quidem** almost a concessive force.

l. 797. haud aliter, *lit.*, ' not otherwise ', = ' even so '. **dubius,** ' perplexed '.

l. 799. quin with **etiam** and the indicative has the sense of ' nay more '. **invaserat,** the pluperfect is used to denote instantaneous action.

l. 800. confusa fuga agmina, ' their ranks routed in flight ' is the object of **vertit. confusa vertit** may be rendered ' he

---

[1] i.e. the historic present. Otherwise it can be rendered as a past.

routed and turned to flight ', the participle and finite verb being equivalent to two finite verbs in the English. See the note on. l. 13.

l. 801. **in unum,** ' together '.

l. 802. **contra** is an adverb. **vires,** ' strength '. **Saturnia Juno.** See the note on l. 2. **audet sufficere.** Supply ' him ' as the indirect object.

l. 804. **germanae,** ' to ·his sister '. Juno was the sister as well as the wife of Jupiter. **haud mollia,** ' not gentle ' = ' stern'.

l. 805. **ni Turnus . . . altis.** The true apodosis of this conditional clause is not quoted but merely implied in the phrase **haud mollia iussa.** The subjunctive **cedat** is due to the protasis being virtually in indirect speech.

l. 806. **iuvenis,** ' the warrior ', i.e. Turnus. **subsistere tantum,** ' to hold his own so strongly (as would be needed) '.

l. 808. **cava tempora circum** : i.e. **circum cava tempora.**

l. 809. **saxis,** ' beneath the stones '. **solida aera,** ' the solid brass ' refers to his helmet which receives such a battering that the metal pieces gape open.

l. 810. **discussae.** Supply **sunt. iubae,** pl. for sing. **capiti,** ' from his head '. **nec sufficit umbo ictibus,** ' and the (shield's) boss does not avail for (=cannot parry) the blows '.

The Oxford Classical Text punctuates this line as follows : **discussaeque iubae, capiti nec sufficit umbo ictibus . . .** The translation will then be : ' his crest was knocked off and the (shield's) boss is of no avail to his head against the blows '. i.e. ' does not protect his head against the blows '. **ictibus** will thus be an abl. of respect.

VOCABULARY

(N.B. In the following vocabulary, the figures (1), (2), (3), (4), after the verbs denote the conjugation. No conjugation number is given in the case of -io verbs like capio).

ā (ab), *prep. with abl.*, from, by.
Abaris, -is, *m.*, Abaris (*a Rutulian slain by Euryalus*).
abditus, -a, -um, hidden.
abdō, -ere, -didī, -ditum (3), hide, bury.
abeō, -īre, -īvī (-iī), -itum, go away, depart.
abiēs, -etis, *f.*, fir-tree ; pine.
abitus, -ūs, *m.*, way out, outlet.
abluō, -ere, -luī, -lūtum (3), wash off.
abrumpō, -ere, -rūpī, -ruptum (3), break off.
absēns, -ntis, absent.
absistō, -ere, -stitī (3), desist.
absum, -esse, āfuī, am absent.
absūmō, -ere, -sūmpsī, -sūmptum (3), take away, destroy.
ac *see* **atque**.
accelerō (1), hasten (to).
accendō, -ere, -cendī, -cēnsum (3), set on fire ; kindle, light.
accingō, -ere, -nxī, -nctum (3), gird on, arm.
acciō, -īre, -cīvī, -cītum (3), summon, send for.
accipiō, -ere, -cēpī, -ceptum, receive ; listen, hear.
accolō, -ere, -coluī(3), dwell near.
ācer, ācris, ācre, keen, eager.
acerbus, -a, -um, bitter.
acernus, -a, -um, of maple wood.

Acesta, -ae, *f.*, Acesta (Segesta, town in Sicily).
Acestes, -is, *m.*, Acestes (*Silician king*).
Achillēs, -is, *m.*, Achilles.
aciēs, -eī, *f.*, line of battle.
ācriter, *adv.*, keenly, eagerly.
Actor, -ōris, *m.*, Actor (*a Trojan*).
āctūtum, *adv.*, immediately.
acuō, -ere, -uī, -ūtum (3), sharpen.
acus, -ūs, *f.*, needle.
ad, *prep. with acc.*, to, towards ; at.
addō, -ere, -didī, -ditum (3), add.
addūcō, -ere, -dūxī, -ductum (3), draw (*to myself*) ; tighten.
(adedō), -ere, -ēdī, -ēsum (3), devour.
adeō, -īre, -īvī (-iī), -itum, go to approach.
adeō, *adv.*, so much *or* very.
adferō, -ferre, attulī, adlātum, bring to.
adfīgō, -ere, -xī, -xum (3), fasten to *or* on ; fix.
adfor (ī) *dep.*, speak to, address.
adgredior, -ī, -gressus, *dep.*, approach, attack.
adhūc, *adv.*, still, as yet.
adigō, -ere, -ēgī, -āctum (3), drive, hurl.
adimō, -ere, -ēmī, -ēmptum (3), take away.

aditus, -ūs, *m.*, approach ; entrance.

adiungō, -ere, -nxī, -nctum (3), join to.

adlābor, -ī, -lapsus (3), *dep.*, glide to ; reach (474).

adloquor, -ī, -locūtus (3), *dep.*, speak to, address.

admittō, -ere, -mīsī, -missum (3), admit.

admoneō (2), warn.

admoveō, -ēre, -mōvī, -mōtum (2), move to.

adnītor, -ī, -nīxus *or* -nīsus (3), *dep.*, lean against ; strive hard.

adnuō, -ere, -uī (3), nod assent ; am favourable to (625).

adsiduē, *adv.*, unceasingly.

adsiduus, -a, -um, unceasing ; ceaseless.

adspīrō (1), breathe upon.

adsuēscō, -ere, -ēvī, -ētum (3), accustom.

adsuētus, -a, -um, accustomed to.

adsum, -esse, -fuī, am here *or* at hand.

adsurgō, -ere, -surrēxī, -surrēctum, (3), rise up *or* to.

adversus, -a, -um, facing, opposite ; adverse.

aeger, -gra, -grum, sick, feeble.

Aeneadēs, -ae, *m.*, son of Aeneas ; *loosely for* Trojan.

Aenēās, -ae, *m.*, Aeneas.

Aenīdes, -ae, *m.*, son of Aeneas.

aēnus, -a, -um, of bronze.

Aeolides, -ae, *m.*, son of Aeolus.

aequō (1), make equal.

aequor, -oris, *n.*, (level surface), *hence* sea *or* plain.

aequus, -a, -um, (level), equal ; fair (56) ; favourable (209), kindly (234).

āēr, āeris, *m.*, air.

aerātus, -a, -um, bronzed, bronze-clad.

āerius, -a, -um, of *or* in the air *or* sky ; heavenly.

aes, aeris, *n.*, bronze.

aetās, -ātis, *f.*, age.

aethēr, -eris, *m.*, upper air, sky.

aetherius, -a, -um, of *or* in the heavens.

aevum, -ī, *n.*, age, life, time.

ager, -grī, *m.*, field.

agger, -eris, *m.*, mound ; rubble (567).

agitō (1), stir, excite.

āgmen, -inis, *n.*, train ; company, troop, host, array (788).

āgnōscō, -ere, -nōvī, -nitum (3), recognise.

āgnus, -ī, *m.*, lamb.

agō, -ere, ēgī, āctum (3), drive, urge on ; do ; lead ; spend (*of time*) ; *imperative* age, agite, come!

agrestis, -e, rustic.

aiō, *defective verb*, say, speak.

āla, -ae, *f.*, wing.

alacer, -cris, -cre, alert, brisk.

Alba, -ae, *f.*, Alba Longa (*town in Latium*).

Albānus, -a, -um, of Alba, Alban ; *as noun*, Albans.

albus, -a, -um, white.

Alcandrus, -ī, *m.*, Alcandrus (*a Trojan*).

Alcānor, -oris, *m.*, Alcanor (*a Trojan*).

āles, -itis, *lit.*, winged : *as noun*, bird.

Alētes, -ae, *m.*, Aletes (*a Trojan*).

aliquis, -quid, some *or* any one, -thing.

aliter, *adv.*, otherwise.

alius, -a, -ud, other, different.

altē, *adv.*, on high.

alter, -era, -erum, the one *or* the other (*of two*) ; second.

altum, -ī, *n.*, the deep sea.

altus, -a, -um, high, deep, lofty, high-piled (325), exalted (697).

alveus, -ī, *m.*, bed (*of a river*).

alvus, -ī, *f.*, belly.

Amāta, -ae, *f.*, Amata (*wife of Latinus*).

ambō, -ae, -ō, both.

āmēns, -ntis, mad, distracted.

amīcus, -ī, *m.*, friend ; *as adj.*, friendly.

ammentum, -ī, *n.*, strap.

amnis, -is, *m.*, river.

amō (1), love, like.

amoenus, -a, -um, pleasant, charming.

amor, -ōris, *m.*, love, longing.

amplius, *comparat. adv.*, more, further ; (any) longer.

amplus, -a, -um, large, great, grand.

Amycus, -ī, *m.*, Amycus (*a Trojan*).

an, *conj.*, or.

Anchīsēs, -ae, *m.*, Anchises (*father of Aeneas*).

angō (3), (squeeze, choke) ; constrain.

anhēlitus, -ūs, *m.*, panting.

anīlis, -e, of an old woman.

anima, -ae, *f.*, breath, life ; soul, spirit.

animal, -ālis, *n.*, living thing ; animal.

animus, -ī, *m.*, mind, spirit, soul ; *in pl.*, spirits, courage.

annōsus, -a, -um, full of years.

annus, -ī, *m.*, year.

ante, *prep. with acc.*, before ; *adv.*, before, first.

Antiphatēs, -ae, *m.*, Antiphates (*a Trojan*).

antīquus, -a, -um, of old, ancient.

anxius, -a, -um, anxious.

aperiō, -īre, -uī, -ertum (4), open ; reveal.

Aphidnus, -ī, *m.*, Aphidnus (*a Trojan*).

Apollō, -inis, *m.*, Apollo.

apparō (1), make ready, prepare.

aptō (1), fit.

aptus, -a, -um, fitted : studded.

Aquīcolus, -ī, *m.*, Aquicolus (*a Trojan*).

aquōsus, -a, -um, watery, rainy.

āra, -ae, *f.*, altar.

arātrum, -ī, *n.*, plough.

Arcēns, -ntis, *m.*, Arcens (*a Sicilian*).

arcus, -ūs, *m.*, bow.

Ardea, -ae, *f.*, Ardea.

ardēns, -ntis, glowing, fiery, eager.

ardeō, -ēre, ārsī (2), burn, blaze, glow, am aglow.

ardor, -ōris, *m.*, heat, glow.

arduus, -a, -um, lofty, aloft, on high ; towering.

argentum, -ī, *n.*, silver.

Argolicus, -a, -um, of Argos, Grecian.

arguō, -ere, -uī, -ūtum (3), make clear, prove.

Arisba, -ae, *f.*, Arisba.

arma, -ōrum, *n. pl.*, arms.

armiger, -erī, *m.*, armour-bearer.

armipotēns, -ntis, powerful in arms ; valiant.

armō (1), arm, equip.

armus, -ī, m., shoulder.

arō (1), plough.

arrēctus, -a, -um, set up on end.

arripiō, -ere, -puī, -eptum, seize, snatch.

ars, artis, f., art, skill.

artus, -ūs, m., limb.

arvum, -ī, n., (ploughed) field; land.

arx, arcis, f., citadel.

Ascanius, -ī, m., Ascanius (son of Aeneas).

ascendō, -ere, -ndī, -nsum (3), climb, mount.

Asīlas, -ae, m., Asilas (a Trojan).

aspectus, -ūs, m., sight.

asper, -era, -erum, rough, cruel ; embossed (263).

aspiciō, -ere, -spēxī, -spectum, look at, behold.

Assaracus, -ī, m., Assaracus.

ast = at.

astō, -āre, -stitī (1), stand by or at.

astrum, -ī, n., star.

at, conj., but.

āter, -tra, -trum, black, dark.

Athesis, -is, m., the Athesis (a river).

atque, conj., and.

Atrīdēs, -ae, m., son of Atreus.

atrōx, -ōcis, fierce.

attingō, -ere, -tigī, -tāctum (3), reach.

attollō, -ere (3), lift up, raise ; reflexive (321) and in pass. (714), rise.

attorqueō, -ēre, -sī, -tum (2), hurl at.

auctor, -ōris, m., author, originator.

audāx, -ācis, bold.

audēns, -ntis, bold.

audeō, -ēre, ausus sum (2), semidep., dare, venture.

audiō (4), hear.

auferō, -ferre, abstulī, ablātum, take or carry off ; rob (443) ; lop off (332).

augeō, -ēre, auxī, auctum (2), increase.

augur, -uris, m., augur, prophet.

augurium, -ī, n., augury.

aula, -ae, f., court-yard, hall.

aura, -ae, f., breeze.

aurātus, -a, -um, gilded.

aureus, -a, -um, golden ; splendid (270).

aurīga -ae, m., charioteer.

auris, -is, m., ear.

Aurōra, -ae, f., the goddess Dawn ; dawn.

aurum, -ī, n., gold.

Ausonia, -ae, f., Ausonia, the land of Italy.

Ausonius, -a, -um, Ausonian (= Italian).

auspicium, -ī, n., augury ; omen.

Auster, -trī, m., the south wind.

ausum, -ī, n., bold deed.

aut, conj., or ; aut . . . aut, either . . . or.

autem, conj., but, yet, however.

auxilium, -ī, n., help, aid.

āvellō, -ere, —, -vulsum or-volsum (3), tear away ; rend asunder.

āversus, -a, -um (turned away), in the rear.

āvertō, -ere, -tī, -sum (3), turn away.

avidus, -a, -um, greedy, eager (for).

avis, -is, f., bird.

āvius, -a, -um, out of the way, remote.

Baiae, -ārum, f. pl., Baiae (*Italian town*).
bālātus, -ūs, m., bleating.
bellātor, -ōris, m., warrior.
bellum, -ī, n., war.
bene, adv., well, good.
Berecyntius, -a, -um, of Mt. Berecyntus, Berecyntine.
biforis, -e, double.
bīnī, -ae, -a, two each, two.
bis, adv., twice.
Bitias, -ae, m., Bitias (*a Trojan*).
bivium, -ī, n., meeting of two roads.
bonus, -a, -um, good.
Boreās, -ae, m., the north wind.
bracchium, -ī, n., arm.
breviter, adv., shortly, briefly.
bulla, -ae, f., boss, stud.
Būtēs, -ae, f., Butes (*a Trojan*).
buxus, -ūs, f. (box-tree) ; flute.

cadō, -ere, cecidī, cāsum (3), fall.
caecus, -a, -um, blind ; hidden, unseen.
caedēs, -is, f., bloodshed, carnage.
Caedicus, -ī, m., Caedicus.
caedō, -ere, cecīdī, caesum (3), slaughter, slay.
caelum, -ī, n., heaven, sky.
Caeneūs, -eī, m., Caeneus (*a Trojan*).
Caīcus, -ī, m., Caicus (*a Trojan*).
callis, -is, m., path, track.
calidus, -a, -um, hot.
cālīgō, -inis, f., darkness.
Calliopē, -ēs, f., Calliope (*a Muse*).
calor, -ōris, m., heat.
campus, -ī, m., plain.

candēns, -ntis, shining, bright, white.
candeō, -ēre, -uī (2), shine, am bright, glisten.
candidus, -a, -um, white ; bright, fair.
canis, -is, c., dog.
cānitiēs, -eī, f., white hair.
canō, -ere, cecinī, cantum (3), sing, utter.
canōrus, -a, -um, melodious, musical.
cantus, -ūs, m., song, tune.
cānus, -a, -um, white-haired.
capessō, -ere, -īvī (-iī), -ītum, seize ; make for (366).
capiō, -ere, cēpī, captum, take, seize.
Capitōlium, -ī, n., the Capitoline hill.
captīvus, -a, -um, captive.
caput, -itis, n., head ; life ; creature.
Capys, -yos, m., Capys (*a Trojan*).
carbasus, -ī, f., *in pl., neut.*, canvas.
cardō, -inis, m., hinge.
careō (2), *often with abl.*, am without.
carīna, -ae, f., keel, ship.
carmen, -inis, n., song, poem.
carpō, -ere, -psī, -ptum (3), pick, pluck ; crop (353).
cārus, -a, -um, dear.
castra, -ōrum, n. pl., camp.
cāsus, -ūs, m., fall, chance, mischance ; fate, fortune.
caterva, -ae, f., troop.
caulae, -ārum, f. pl., sheepfold.
causa, -ae, f., cause, reason.
cautes, -is, f., rock.
cavus, -a, -um, hollow.

cēdō, -ere, cessī, cessum (3), yield, withdraw, depart.

celer, -eris, -ere, swift.

celerō (1), speed, hasten.

cēlō (1), hide, conceal.

centēnī, -ae, -a, a hundred each.

centum, a hundred.

cerebrum, -ī, n., brain.

cernō, -ere, crēvī, crētum (3), see, observe.

certāmen, -inis, n., contest, struggle.

certō (1), contend, struggle; strive.

certus, -a, -um, determined, resolute, settled; sure.

cervīx, -īcis, f., neck.

cervus, -ī, m., stag.

cēterus, -a, -um, other, remaining; the rest of.

ceu, conj., like, as.

chlamys, -ydis, f., scarf, mantle.

chorea, -ae, f., dance.

chorus, -ī, m., dance; troop, band.

cieō, -ēre, cīvī, citum (2), rouse.

cingō, -ere, -nxī, -nctum (3), encircle, surround, wreathe.

cingula, -ōrum, n., pl., belt.

cinis, -eris, m., mostly in pl., ashes, embers.

circum, adv., and prep. with acc., around.

circumdō, -dare, -dedī, -datum (1), put or set around; surround, gird (462).

circumspiciō, -ere, -spēxī, -spectum, look around.

cithara, -ae, f., lyre.

citus, -a, -um, quick.

cīvis, -is, c., citizen.

clāmō (1), shout.

clāmor, -ōris, m., shout, cry.

clārus, -a, -um, bright; clear; famous.

classis, -is, f., fleet.

claudō, -ere, -sī, -sum (3), shut, shut in.

claustrum, -ī, n., bar, bolt.

clipeus, -ī, m., shield.

Clonius, -ī, m., Clonius (a Trojan).

Clytius, -ī, m., Clytius (a Trojan).

coeō, -īre, -īvī (-iī), -itum, come together, gather.

coeptum, -ī, n., beginning, undertaking.

coerceō (2), hold together, command (27).

cōgnōmen, -inis, n., surname.

cōgnōscō, -ere, -nōvī, -gnitum (3), learn.

cōgō, -ere, coēgī, coāctum (3), collect, muster.

cohibeō (2), confine.

colligō, -ere, -lēgī, -lēctum (3), collect, muster; rally (689).

collum, -ī, n., neck.

color, -ōris, m., colour, hue.

coma, -ae, f., hair.

comes, -itis, c., companion.

comitor (1), dep., accompany.

comminus, adv., hand to hand; at close quarters.

commisceō, -ēre, -miscuī, -mīxtum (-mīstum) (2), mix or mingle together.

committō, -ere, -mīsī, -mīssum (3), entrust.

commoveō, -ēre, -mōvī, -mōtum (2) stir, shake, rouse.

commūnis, -e, shared, common.

compellō (1), address.

complector, -ī, -plexus (3), dep., embrace.

compleō, -ēre, -ēvī, -ētum (2), fill, fulfil (108).

compōnō, -ere, -posuī, -positum (3), put together, settle.

comportō (1), bring together.

concēdō, -ere, -cessī, -cessum (3), yield, grant.

concieō, -ēre, -cīvī, -citum (2), rouse, excite, provoke.

concipiō, -ere, -cēpī, -ceptum, conceive, shape.

conclāmō (1), shout or cry aloud.

concursus, -ūs, m., rush, throng, concourse.

concutiō, -ere, -cussī, -cussum, shake or strike violently.

condō, -ere, -didī, -ditum (3), hide, bury.

cōnferō, -ferre, -tulī, -lātum, bring together ; manum conferre (44) to fight.

cōnfestim, adv., immediately, forthwith.

cōnfīgō, -ere, -fīxī, -fīxum (3), pierce through ; transfix.

cōnfodiō, -ere, -fōdī, -fossum, pierce or stab through.

cōnfundō, -ere, -fūdī, -fūsum (3), confuse, disorder, rout.

cōniciō, -ere, -iēcī, -iectum, hurl.

cōnītor, -ī, -nīsus or -nīxus (3), dep., struggle, strain.

coniunx, -iugis, c., husband, wife.

conlābor, -ī, -lapsus (3), dep., fall, sink.

conlūceō (2), gleam, am lit up.

cōnor (1), dep., try, attempt.

cōnscius, -a, -um, conscious, aware of.

cōnserō, -ere, -seruī, -sertum (3), join; dextram cōnserere, to fight hand to hand, join battle (741).

cōnsīdō, -ere, -sēdī, -sessum (3), settle, sink.

cōnsilium, -ī, n., plan ; counsel.

cōnsistō, -ere, -stitī, -stitum (3), stand, halt.

cōnspectus, -ūs, m., sight.

cōnspiciō, -ere, -spēxī, -spectum, catch sight of, descry.

cōnstruō, -ere, -ūxī, -ūctum (3), erect, build.

cōnsulō, -ere, -luī, -ltum (3), consult.

cōnsurgō, -ere, -surrēxī, -surrēctum (3), rise up, arise.

contemptor, -ōris, m., he who disregards or scorns.

contendō, -ere, -dī, -tum (3), strive, contend.

contentus, -a, -um, content.

conterreō (2), terrify, frighten.

conticēscō, -ere, -ticuī (3), become silent.

contingō, -ere, -tigī, -tāctum (3), happen ; fall to.

continuō, adv., forthwith.

contorqueō, -ēre, -rsī, -rtum (2), hurl.

contrā, adv. and prep. with acc., against ; in reply.

contrarius, -a, -um, opposite; contrary.

contus, -ī, m., pole.

cōnūbium, -ī, n., marriage.

conveniō, -īre, -vēnī, -ventum (4), assemble.

convertō, -ere, -tī, -sum (3), turn.

cōpia, -ae, f., means, opportunity.

cor, cordis, n., heart, mind.

cornu, -ūs, n., horn ; bow.

cornus, -ī, f. (cornel cherry tree); javelin or spear (of that tree).

corōna, -ae, *f.*, garland ; ring (508, 551).

corōnō (1), garland ; surround (380).

corpus, -oris, *n.*, body.

corripiō, -ere, -ripuī, -reptum, seize, catch, snatch up.

cortex, -icis, *m.*, bark.

coruscus, -a, -um, bright, glittering.

Corynaeus, -ī, *m.*, Corynaeus (*a Rutulian*).

Corythus, -ī, *m.*, Corythus.

costa, -ae, *f.*, rib.

crātēr, -ēris, *m.*, mixing-bowl.

crēdō, -ere, -didī, -ditum (3), trust in, believe ; entrust.

crēscō, -ere, crēvī, crētum (3), grow.

Crētheūs, -eī, *m.*, Cretheus (*a Trojan*).

Creūsa, -ae, *f.*, Creusa (*wife of Aeneas*).

crīnis, -is, *m.*, hair.

crīnītus, -a, -um, long-haired.

crista, -ae, *f.*, crest.

croceus, -a, -um, saffron-coloured.

crocus, -ī, *m.*, saffron.

crūdēlis, -e, cruel.

crūdus, -a, -um, raw ; undressed, unpeeled (743).

cruentus, -a, -um, bloody.

cruor, -ōris, *m.*, blood, gore.

cubīle, -is, *n.*, bed.

cum, *conj.*, when, since.

cum, *prep. with abl.*, with.

cunctor (1), *dep.*, hesitate, tarry.

cūnctus, -a, -um, all, one and all.

cupīdō, -inis, *f.*, desire.

cupiō, -ere, -īvī, -ītum, desire.

cūra, -ae, *f.*, care, anxiety.

cūrō (1), care for, care.

currus, -ūs, *m.*, chariot, car.

cursus, -ūs, *m.*, running ; course.

custōdia, -ae, *f.*, (a watching) ; watch ; the watch ; guards (166).

custōdiō (4), guard.

custōs, -ōdis, *c.*, guard.

cycnus, -ī, *m.*, swan.

Danaus, -a, -um, Greek : *as noun in pl.*, the Greeks.

Dardanidae, -ārum, *m. pl., lit.*, sons of Dardanus, i.e. Trojans.

Dardanius, -a, -um, Trojan.

dē, *prep. with abl.*, down from, from ; about, concerning, of.

dea, -ae, *f.*, goddess.

dēbeō (2), owe, ought.

dēbilitō (1), weaken.

dēbitus, -a, -um, due.

dēcēdō, -ere, -cessī, -cessum (3), withdraw.

decorō (1), adorn, honour.

decōrus, -a, -um, comely, becoming, adorned.

decimus, -a, -um, tenth.

decus, -oris, *n.*, grace, beauty ; glory, renown (405).

dēfendō, -ere, -dī, -nsum (3), ward off, defend.

dēferō, -ferre, -tulī, -lātum, bring down ; bring (news) ; report.

dēficiō, -ere, -fēcī, -fectum, fail, wane.

dēfungor, -ī, -fūnctus (3), *dep.*, fulfil.

dēgō, -ere, dēgī (3), spend, pass.

dehinc, *adv.*, hence, next.

dēiciō, -ere, -iēcī, -iectum, throw down, dislodge ; sever (770).

dēinde, *adv.*, next.

dēleō, -ēre, -ēvī, -ētum (2), destroy.

dēligō, -ere, -lēgī, -lēctum (3), choose.

delphīn, -īnis, *m.*, dolphin.

dēmēns, -ntis, mad, infatuated.

dementia, -ae, *f.*, madness, infatuation.

dēmergō, -ere, -sī, -sum (3), plunge, dip (119) ; sink.

dēmittō, -ere, -mīsī, -mīssum (3), send *or* let down, drop (437).

dēmum, *adv.*, at last.

dēnsus, -a, -um, thick, close ; serried (551, 788).

dēpellō, -ere, -pulī, -pulsum (3), drive *or* send off *or* away.

dēsecō, -āre, -secuī, -sectum (1), cut off.

dēserō, -ere, -ruī, -rtum (3), desert, leave behind.

dēsidia, -ae, *f.*, sloth.

dēsum, -esse, -fuī, am wanting.

dēsuper, *adv.*, from above.

dētorqueō, -ēre, -sī, -tum (2), turn away, bend.

dētrūdō, -ere, -sī, -sum (3), thrust down.

deus, -ī, *m.*, god.

dēvincō, -ere, -vīcī, -vīctum (3), overcome, subdue.

dexter, -era, -erum, on the right.

dextra, -ae, *f.*, the right hand.

dīcō, -ere, -xī, -ctum (3), say ; speak.

dictum, -ī, *n.*, saying, word.

Dīdō, -ōnis, *f.*, Dido (*Queen of Carthage*).

diēs, -eī, *m. and f.*, day.

differō, -ferre, distulī, dīlātum, put off.

diffindō, -ere, -fidī, -fissum (3), split.

diffugiō, -ere, -fūgī, flee in different directions ; scatter.

dignus, -a, -um, *often with abl.*, worthy (of), fitting (252).

dīligō, -ere, -lēxī, -lēctum (3), love.

dīmoveō, -ēre, -mōvī, -mōtum (2), move ; part, dislodge.

Dindyma, -ōrum, *n. pl.*, Dindyma (*a mountain*).

Dioxippus -ī, *m.*, Dioxippus (*a Trojan*).

Dīra, -ae, *f.*, fury.

dīripiō, -ere, -uī, -eptum, plunder, strip.

dīrus, -a, -um, dreadful.

discēdō, -ere, -cessī, -cessum (3), leave, depart.

discerpō, -ere, -psī, -ptum (3), scatter.

discors, -dis, at variance, discordant.

discrīmen, -inis, *n.*, separation; hazard (210).

discurrō, -ere, -currī, -cursum (3), run to and fro.

discutiō, -ere, -cussī, -cussum (3), strike asunder, shatter ; dispel.

dissimilis, -e, unlike.

dītissimus, *superlat*, of dīves.

dīva, -ae, *f.*, goddess.

dīverberō (1), strike asunder, cleave.

dīversus, -a, -um, in different directions ; different, various.

dīves, -itis, rich.

dīvidō, -ere, -sī, -sum (3), divide.

dīvīnus, -a, -um, divine.

dīvortium, -ī, *n.*, (separation) ; fork.

dīvus, -a, -um, divine ; *as noun*, a god.

dō, dare, dedī, datum (1), give, grant; shed (*of tears*, 292).

doceō, -ēre, -uī, -ctum (2), teach.

doleō (2), grieve, am indignant.

dolor, -ōris, *m.*, pain, pang, agony (426) ; rage, resentment.

dolus, -ī, *m.*, deceit, guile ; treachery.

dominus, -ī, *m.*, owner, lord.

domitor, -ōris, *m.*, tamer, trainer.

domō, -āre, -uī, -itum (1) subdue.

domus, -ūs, *f.*, house, home.

donec, *conj.*, until.

dōnō, (1), give.

dōnum, -ī, *n.*, gift.

dōtālis, -e, of a dowry.

Dōtō, -ūs, *f.*, Doto (*a sea-nymph*).

dubitō (1), hesitate ; think of (191).

dubius, -a, -um, doubtful.

dūcō, -ere, -xī, -ctum (3), lead ; spend (*of time* 166).

ductor, -ōris, *m.*, leader, captain.

dulcis, -e, sweet, dear.

dum, *conj.*, while, until.

dūmus, -ī, *m.*, *only in pl.*, thicket.

duo, -ae, -o, two.

duplex, -icis, two-fold, double ; two (16).

dūrō (1), harden.

dūrus, -a, -um, hard ; cruel.

dux, ducis, *m.*, leader.

e(=ex), *prep. with abl.*, out of, from.

eburnus, -a, -um, of ivory.

ecce, *interject.*, lo! see!

ecquis, -quae (-qua), -quid, any one?

edō, -ere (esse), ēdī, ēsum (3), eat.

ēdō, -ere, -didī, -ditum (3), give forth ; deal (527).

ēdūcō, -ere, -xī, -ctum (3), lead forth *or* out : rear.

efferō, -ferre, extulī, ēlātum, bring forth, lift (817).

effor (1), *dep.*, speak forth *or* out.

effugiō, -ere, -fūgī, get away ; escape.

effulgeō, -ēre, -sī (2), gleam *or* blaze forth.

effundō, -ere, -fūdī, -fūsum (3), pour out *or* forth.

egeō (2), *with abl. or gen.*, need.

ego, meī, I.

ēgredior, -ī, -gressus, go forth, leave.

ēgregius, -a, -um, distinguished, noble.

ēiciō, -ere, -iēci, -iectum, cast out *or* forth.

ēlābor, -ī, -lapsus (*dep.*) (glide forth) ; escape.

Ēmathion, -onis, *m.*, Emathion (*a Trojan*).

ēmicō, -āre, -cuī (1) shoot out *or* forth ; leap up *or* forward (736).

ēmittō, -ere, -mīsī, -missum (3), send forth, launch (52).

emō, -ere, ēmī, ēmptum (3), buy.

ēn, *interject.* lo! behold!

enim, *conj.*, for.

ēnsis, -is, *m.*, sword.

eō, īre, iī (īvī), itum, go ; stalk (597).

eōdem, *adv.*, to the same place.

eques, -itis, *m.*, horseman.

equidem, *adv.*, truly, indeed.

equīnus, -a, -um, of a horse.

equus, -ī, *m.*, horse.

ergō, *adv.*, therefore, so.

ērigō, -ere, -rēxī, -rēctum (3), set up, erect.

ēripiō, -ere, -puī, -ptum, snatch from *or* away ; seize ; rescue.

errō (1), wander.

ērudiō (4), train, teach, rear.

Erymas, -ntis, *m.*, Erymas (*a Trojan*).

et, *conj.*, and ; *adv.*, too, also.

etiam, *adv.*, also.

Etruscus, -a, -um, Etruscan ; *as noun*, an Etruscan.

etsī, *conj.*, even if, although.

Euander, -drī, *m.*, Evander.

Euboicus, -a, -um, Euboean, of Euboea.

Euryalus, -ī, *m.*, Euryalus (*a Trojan*).

ēvādō, -ere, -sī, sum (3), escape from.

ēvānēscō, -ere, -nuī (3), vanish, die away.

ēvertō, -ere, -tī, -sum (3), overturn.

ēvolō (1), fly out *or* away.

ēvolvō, -ere, -vī, -volūtum (3), roll forth ; unroll.

ex, *see* ē.

exaestuō (1), boil up, are in ferment.

exanimis, -e, lifeless.

excēdō, -ere, -cessī, -cessum (3), withdraw.

excidō, -ere, -cidī (3), fall out.

excipiō, -ere, -cēpī, -ceptum, receive ; take up (54) ; break in, answer (258) ; take apart (271).

excitō (1), rouse, awaken.

exclūdō, -ere, -sī, -sum (3), shut out.

excubiae, -ārum, *f. pl.*, watching, watchmen.

excubō, -āre, -uī, -itum (1), keep watch.

excutiō, -ere, -cussī, -cussum, shake from.

exeō, -īre, -iī, -itum, go *or* come forth.

exerceō (2), keep busy.

exercitus, -ūs, *m.*, host, army.

exhauriō, -īre, -hausī, -haustum (4), drain.

exiguus, -a, -um, small, scanty.

eximō, -ere, -ēmī, -ēmptum (3), take away, remove.

exitium, -ī, *n.*, destruction.

explōrō (1), examine ; test.

exposcō, -ere, -poposcī (3), entreat.

expūgnō (1), storm.

exsanguis, -e, bloodless, lifeless.

exscindō, -ere, -scidī, -scissum (3), root out, destroy.

exspectō (1), await.

exstruō, -ere, -xī, -ctum (3), build up, rear, raise (326).

extendō, -ere, -dī, -sum (3), stretch out.

exterritus, -a, -um, frightened, terrified.

extrēmus, -a, -um, furthest, last.

exuō, -ere, -uī, -ūtum (3), put *or* take off, doff.

exūrō, -ere, -ussī, -ūstum (3), burn up.

exuviae, -ārum, *f. pl.*, anything stripped off (307) ; spoils.

fabricō (1), fashion.

facēssō, -ere, -cēssī, -cēssītum (3), perform, execute.

faciēs, -ēī, *f.*, appearance, form, face.

facilis, -e, easy.

faciō, -ere, fēcī, factum, make, do.

factum, -ī, n., deed.

Fādus, -ī, m., Fadus (a Rutulian).

fallāx, -ācis, treacherous.

fallō, -ere, fefellī, falsum (3), deceive.

fāma, -ae, f., fame, reputation.

famēs, -is, f., hunger.

famulus, -ī, m., servant.

fās, n. indeclin., divine law, right.

fastīgium, -ī, n., gable, pediment (408) ; roof (568).

fātālis, -e, fated.

fateor, -ērī, fassus (2), dep., confess.

fātifer, -era, -erum, death-dealing.

fatīgō (1), tire out.

fatīscō, -ere, fall apart, gape.

fātum, -ī, n., fate, destiny.

faucēs, -ium, f. pl., throat.

favilla, -ae, f., ashes.

fax, facis, f., torch, fire-brand.

fēlīx, -īcis, fortunate ; skilled (772).

fēmina, -ae, f., woman.

fēmineus, -a, -um, of women.

fenestra, -ae, f., window ; loophole (534).

fera, -ae, f., wild beast.

ferō, ferre, tulī, lātum, bear, bring, carry ; carry away (354) ; produce (249).

ferōx, -ōcis, fierce.

ferrūgō, -inis, f. (rust) ; purple (582).

ferrum, -ī, n., iron ; sword.

fertilis, -e, fertile.

ferus, -a, -um, wild, untamed, savage.

ferveō (2), am hot, inflamed, agitated.

fervidus, -a, -um, hot ; fiery, impetuous, hasty.

fessus, -a, -um, weary.

festīnus, -a, -um, hasty, in haste.

festus, -a, -um, festive, joyful.

fībula, -ae, f., brooch, pin.

fictor, -ōris, m., fashioner.

fidēlis, -e, faithful, trusty.

fidēs, -ēī, f., faith, trust.

fīdō, -ere, fīsūs sum (3), semi-dep., often with abl., trust (in).

fīdūcia, -ae, f., confidence.

fīdus, -a, -um, loyal, faithful.

fīgō, -ere, -īxī, -xum (3), pierce.

fīlius, -ī, m., son.

findō, -ere, —, fissum (3), split, cleave : fissus (413), broken.

fingō, -ere, -nxī, -ctum (3), (mould) : shape, invent.

fīnis, -is, m. or f., end ; territory.

fīō, fierī, factus, am made, become.

fīrmō (1), strengthen.

flagrō (1), blaze, burn.

flāmen, -inis, n., breeze, blast.

flamma, -ae, f., flame ; in pl., watchfires (160).

flāvus, -a, -um, yellow.

flectō, -ere, -xī, -xum (3), bend ; guide (606).

fleō, -ēre, flēvī, flētum (2), weep ; weep (for).

flētus, -ūs, m., weeping.

(flictus), -ūs, m., only in abl., striking, clashing.

flōs, flōris, m., flower.

flūmen, -inis, n., river.

fluō, -ere, -xī, -xum (3), flow ; drip (472).

fluviālis, -e, of a river.

fluvius, -ī, m., stream.

focus, -ī, m., hearth, fire.

[for], fārī (1) *dep.*, speak, say.
fōrma, -ae, *f.*, bearing ; shape, figure.
formīdō, -inis, *f.*, fear, dread.
fōrmō (1), form, shape, build (80).
fōrte, by chance.
fortis, -e, brave, strong, stout.
fōrtūna, -ae, *f.*, fortune, luck: chance.
fōrtūnātus, -a, -um, happy, fortunate.
fossa, -ae, *f.*, ditch.
foveō, -ēre, fōvī, fōtum (2) (keep warm) ; cherish, hug (57).
frāgmen, -inis, *n.*, fragment.
fragor, -ōris, *m.*, crash.
frangō, -ere, frēgī, frāctum (3), break.
frāter, -tris, *m.*, brother.
frāternus, -a, -um, of a brother, brotherly.
fraus, fraudis, *f.*, deceit, guile.
fremitus, -ūs, *m.*, murmur, clamour, roar.
fremō, -ere, -uī, -itum (3), murmur ; roar, rage.
frētus, -a, -um, *often with abl.*, relying on.
frīgidus, -a, -um, cold.
frōns, frontis, *f.*, forehead, brow.
frūstrā, *adv.*, in vain.
fuga, -ae, *f.*, flight : personified (719).
fugāx, -ācis, flying.
fugiō, -ere, fūgī, flee, fly.
fulgeō, -ēre, -sī (2), shine, glitter.
fulmen, -inis, *n.*, lightning ; thunderbolt.
fulmineus, -a, -um, like lightning, flashing.
fūmidus, -a, -um, smoky.

fūmifer, -era, -erum, smoke bearing.
fūmus, -ī, *m.*, smoke.
funda, -ae, *f.*, sling.
fundō, -ere, fūdī, fūsum (3), pour, pour forth ; lay low (592) ; vanquish (722).
fūnus, -eris, *n.*, funeral ; death.
furō (3), rage, am frenzied.
furor, -ōris, *m.*, frenzy, madness.
fūrtim, *adv.*, by stealth.
fūrtum, -ī, *n.*, theft.

Galateā, -ae, *f.*, Galatea (*a sea-nymph*).
galea, -ae, *f.*, helmet.
Ganges, -is, *m.*, Ganges (*a river*).
gelu, -ūs, *m.*, cold, frost.
geminus, -a, -um, twin ; pair of.
gemitus, -ūs, *m.*, groaning, sighing.
genetrīx, -īcis, *f.*, mother.
genitor, -ōris, *m.*, father; = Jupiter (630).
gēns, gentis, *f.*, race.
genus, -eris, *n.*, race, line *or* lineage ; family (302).
germāna, -ae, *f.*, sister.
germānus, -ī, *m.*, brother.
gerō, -ere, gessī, gestum (3), carry, carry on ; wear.
gīgnō, -ere, genuī, genitum (3), bear, beget.
gladius, -ī, *m.*, sword.
globus, -ī, *m.*, mass, band.
glomerō (1), mass : huddle (539) ; *in pass.*, mass *or* gather together (689).
glōria, -ae, *f.*, glory.
Gnōsius, -a, -um, Cretan.
gradior, -ī, gressus, *dep.*, walk, go.
grāmen, -inis, *n.*, grass.

grandō, -inis, *f.*, hail.

grātia, -ae, *f.*, favour, influence ; honour (298).

grātus, -a, -um, pleasing.

gravis, -e, heavy.

gravō (1), weigh down.

gremium, -ī, *n.*, bosom ; care (261).

gurges, -itis, *m.*, (deep) sea ; flood.

Gȳges, -is, *m.*, *acc.*, Gȳgen, Gyges (*a Trojan*).

habēna, -ae, *f.*, thong.

habeō (2), have, possess ; hold ; consider.

habilis, -e (for holding), handy, well-fitting.

hāc, *adv.*, by this way, here.

haedus, -ī, *m.*, kid.

Haemon, -ōnis, *m.*, Haemon (*a Rutulian*).

haereō, -ēre, -sī, -sum (2), stick (fast).

Halius, -ī, *m.*, Halius (*a Trojan*).

Halys, -yos, *m.*, Halys (*a Trojan*).

harēna, -ae, *f.*, sand.

hasta, -ae, *f.*, spear, lance.

hastīle, -is, *n.*, spear, javelin.

haud, *adv.*, not, no.

hauriō, -īre, -sī, -stum (4), drain.

Hector, -oris, *m.*, Hector (*son of Priam*).

heia, *interjection*, ho!

Helēnor, -oris, *m.*, Helenor (*a Trojan*).

herba, - ae, *f.*, grass.

Herbēsus, -ī, *m.*, Herbesus (*a Rutulian*).

heu, *interject.*, alas!

Hibērus, -a, -um, Spanish.

hīc, haec, hōc, this ; he, she, it, they.

hīc, *adv.*, here, hereupon.

hiems, -is, *f.*, winter ; tempest (671).

hinc, *adv.*, hence, from here *or* there ; hinc . . . hinc, on this side . . . on that.

homō, -inis, *m. or f.*, a human being, a man.

honōs, -ōris, *m.*, honour, glory.

horrēns, -ntis, shaggy, rough.

horreō (2), (am rough) ; shudder at ; horrendus, -a, -um, dreadful, awful.

horridus, -a, -um, rough, bristling.

horrisonus, -a, -um, resounding terribly.

hospitium, -ī, *n.*, hospitality, bond of friendship (361).

hostis, -is, *c.*, foe, enemy.

hūc, *adv.*, hither : huc . . . illuc, this way and that.

humus, -ī, *f.*, ground, earth ; *loc.*, humī, on *or* to the ground.

Hyrtacidēs, -ae, *m.* (*patronymic*), son of Hyrtacus.

Hyrtacus, -ī, *m.*, Hyrtacus (*father of Nisus*).

iaceō (2), lie.

iaciō, -ere, iēcī, iactum, throw, hurl.

iactō (1), throw, toss ; boast (134).

iaculum, -ī, *n.*, dart, javelin.

Iaera, -ae, *f.*, Iaera (*wood-nymph*).

iam, *adv.*, now, already.

iamdudum, *adv.*, for a long time now.

ibi, *adv.*, there.

ictus, -ūs, *m.*, blow, stroke.

Īda, -ae, *f.*, (i), Ida (*mountain near Troy*) ; (ii) Ida (*mother of Nisus*).

Īdaeus, -a, -um, of Ida.

Īdaeus, -ī, m., Idaeus (a Trojan).

Īdas, -ae, m., Idas (a Trojan).

īdem, eadem, idem, the same.

igitur, adv., therefore.

īgnārus, -a, -um, ignorant (of).

īgnēscō (3), take fire, burn.

īgnis, -is, m., fire, watchfire (166).

īgnōtus, -a, -um, unknown, strange.

īlex, -icis, f., holm-oak.

īlia, -ium, n. pl., flank, groin.

Īlioneūs, -eī, m., Ilioneus (a Trojan).

Īlius, -a, -um, of Ilium, i.e. of Troy.

ille, illa, illud, that; he, she, it; they.

illūc, adv., thither, there.

īmāgō, -inis, f., likeness, picture.

imber, -bris, m., rain.

immānis, -e, huge, vast, enormous; ghastly (751).

immemor, -ōris, unmindful, forgetful.

immineō (2), hang over, threaten.

immittō, -ere, -mīsī, -missum (3), send into, hurl; let slip (719); se immittere, to dash.

immō, adv., on the contrary; nay rather.

immōbilis, -e, immovable.

immortālis, -e, immortal.

impāstus, -a, -um, unfed, hungry.

impediō (4), hinder, entangle.

impellō, -ere, -pulī, -pulsum (3), drive on.

imperium, -ī, n., sway, command.

impleō, -ēre, -plēvī, -plētum (2), fill.

impōnō, -ere, -posuī, -positum (3), put or place on.

imprōbus, -a, -um, shameless; reckless (62).

improperātus, -a, -um, unhurried, deliberate.

imprōvīsus, -a, -um, unforeseen, unexpected.

imprūdēns, -ntis, unawares.

impūbēs, -eris, or -is, m., (beardless); youthful, boyish.

impūnē, adv., with impunity; unavenged (653).

īmus, -a, -um, lowest, bottom of.

in, prep. with abl., in or on; with acc., into, onto, to, for.

inānis, -e, empty; idle (219).

Īnarimē, -ēs, f., Inarime (an island).

incēdō, -ere, -cessī, -cessum (3), advance, stalk or march forward.

incendium, -ī, n., fire, conflagration.

incendō, -ere, -dī, -nsum (3), set on fire; kindle (500); incēnsus, perf. part. pass., roused, excited, fired with passion.

inceptum, -ī, n., attempt, undertaking.

incertus, -a, -um, uncertain.

incidō, -ere, -cidī (3), fall in or on.

incipiō, -ere, -cēpī, -ceptum, begin.

inclūdō, -ere, -sī, -sum (3), shut in.

increpō, -āre, -uī, -itum (1), chide, taunt (560); ring out (504).

incrēscō, -ere, -ēvī (3), grow, increase.

incumbō, -ere, -cubuī, -cubitum (3), press on, set to work.

indīgnus, -a, -um, unworthy: (sometimes with abl.).

indulgeō, -ēre, -sī, -ltum (2), indulge, allow.

induō, -ere, -uī, -ūtum (3), don, put on.

iners, -rtis, shiftless, sluggish, craven (55).

infēlīx, -īcis, luckless, hapless, unhappy.

infēnsus, -a, -um, hostile ; threatening : angry.

inferiae, -ārum, f. pl., sacrifices or offerings in honour of the dead.

inferō, -ferre, -tulī, illātum, bring in ; hurl at.

infestus, -a, -um, deadly, dangerous.

infīgō, -ere, -fīxī, -fīxum (3), fix in or on.

inflammō (1), kindle, inflame.

inflectō, -ere, -flēxī, -flexum (3), bend.

infringō, -ere, -frēgī, -frāctum (3), break down ; blunt (499).

infundō, -ere, -fūdī, -fūsum (3), pour on.

ingeminō (1), redouble.

ingēns, -ntis, huge, vast, enormous.

ingerō, -ere, -gessī, -gestum (3), throw or heap or hurl upon.

inglōrius, -a, -um, unknown to fame.

iniciō, -ere, -iēcī, -iectum, throw or cast in or on to.

inimīcus, -a, -um, hostile.

inīquus, -a, -um, uneven ; unfair, unpropitious.

iniūria, -ae, f., wrong, outrage.

inlacrimō (1), shed tears at or over.

inlīdō, -ere, -līsī, -līsum (3), dash into.

inlūdō, -ere, -sī, -sum (3), mock at.

inops, -opis, helpless, in need : powerless.

inquam, -is, -it, -iunt, defect vb., say.

inritus, -a, -um, in vain.

inrumpō, -ere, -rūpī, -ruptum (3), break or burst in.

inruō, -ere, -uī (3), rush in or against.

insalūtātus, -a, -um, without a greeting or a farewell.

insānus, -a, -um, mad.

insequor, -ī, -secūtus (3), dep., follow upon.

insidiae, -ārum, f. pl., ambush.

insidior (1), dep., lie in wait, plot mischief (against) with dat.

insīgnis, -e, conspicuous, prominent, noble.

insomnis, -e, sleepless.

instō, -āre, -stitī, -statum (1) press or close upon.

instruō, -ere, -uī, -ctum (3), arrange, draw up.

insuper, adv., above, from above : prep. with abl., in addition to.

insurgō, -ere, -surrēxī, -surrēctum (3), rise on.

integer, -gra, -grum, whole, unimpaired.

intendō, -ere, -dī, -tum or -sum (3), stretch ; aim (623) ; bend (665).

inter, prep. with acc., among, between.

intereā, adv., meanwhile.

interior, -ius, inner.

interlūceō, -ēre, -lūxī (2), shows light.

interrumpō, -ere, -rūpī, -ruptum (3), break through.

intonō, -āre, -uī (1), thunder.

intōnsus, -a, -um, unshorn, un-
shaved.

intorqueō, -ēre, -torsī, -tortum
(2), hurl at *or* in.

intrā, *prep. with acc.*, within.

intus, *adv.*, within.

invādō, -ere, -vāsī, -vāsum
(3), attack ; attempt (186).

inveniō, -īre, -vēnī, -ventum (4),
find.

invideō, -ēre, -vīdī, -vīsum (2),
am envious *or* jealous, grudge
(655), *with dat.*

invigilō (1), am awake over.

invīsus, -a, -um, hated.

invītō (1), invite.

invitus, -a, -um, unwilling.

invius, -a, -um, impassable.

ipse, -a, -um, -self ; he himself
etc. ; very.

īra, -ae, *f.*, anger.

Īris, -idis, *f.*, Iris.

is, ea, id, that, this ; *also as pro-
noun*, he, she, it, they.

iste, -a, -ud, that (*of yours*).

ita, *adv.*, so.

Ītalia, -ae, *f.*, Italy.

Ītalus, -a, -um, Italian ; *also as
noun*, an Italian.

iter, itineris, *n.*, journey, way,
route.

iterum, *adv.*, for a second time,
again.

Itys, -yos, *m.*, Itys (*a Trojan*).

iuba, -ae, *f.*, mane, crest, plume.

iubeō, -ēre, iussī, -iūssum (2),
order, command, give orders.

Iūlus, -ī, *m.*, Iulus (*son of
Aeneas*).

iungō, -ere, -nxī, -nctum (3), join ;
unite (361).

Iūnō, -ōnis, *f.*, Juno (*sister and
wife of Jupiter*).

Iuppiter, Iovis, *m.*, Jupiter, Jove.

iūrō (1), swear.

iūs, iūris, *n.*, right ; iūre ; rightly,
deservedly.

iūssum, -ī, *n.*, command.

iuvencus, -ī, *m.*, steer, bullock.

iuvenis, -is, *m.*, young man,
warrior.

iuventa, -ae, *f.*, youth.

iuventūs, -tūtīs, *f.*, youth, war-
riors, chivalry.

iuvō, -āre, iūvī, iūtum (1), help ;
impersonally, it delights, it is a
pleasure.

iūxtā, *adv., and prep. with acc.*,
near, close to.

labor, -ōris, *m.*, labour, work, toil,
effort (404).

lacer, -era, -erum, mangled.

lacertus, -ī, *m.*, arm.

lacrima, -ae, *f.*, tear.

lacrimō (1), weep, shed tears.

laetitia, -ae, *f.*, joy, gladness.

laetus, -a, -um, glad, joyful,
happy.

laeva, -ae, *f.*, left hand.

laevus, -a, -um, on the left.

lampas, -adis, *f.*, torch.

Lamus, -ī, *m.*, Lamus (*a Rutu-
lian*).

Lamyrus, -ī, *m.*, Lamyrus (*a
Rutulian*).

languēscō, -ere, -guī (3), droop.

lapsus, -ūs, *m.*, gliding, course.

Lār, Laris, *m.*, Lar (*household
god*).

lassus, -a, -um, wearied, faint.

lātē, *adv.*, far and wide.

lateō (2), lie hid.

Latīnus, -a, -um, of Latium, Latin ; *as noun,* a Latin.

Latīnus, -ī, *m.,* Latinus (*king of Lavinium*).

Lātōnius, -a, -um, of Latona.

latus, -eris, *n.,* side.

lātus, -a, -um, wide, broad.

Laurentius, -a, -um, of Laurentum.

laus, laudis, *f.,* praise ; renown ; glorious deed.

Lavīnius, -a, -um, of Lavinium.

lavō, -āre, lāvī, lavātum *or* **lautum** (1), wash.

laxō (1), loosen, relax.

legiō, -ōnis, *f.,* levy ; army.

legō, -ere, lēgī, lēctum (3), choose ; *perfect part. pass.,* **lēctus,** chosen, picked.

leō, -ōnis, *m.,* lion.

lepus, -oris, *m.,* hare.

lētālis, -e, deadly, fatal.

lētum, -ī, *n.,* death.

levis, -e, light ; light-armed.

lībrō (1), poise, level.

licet (2), *impersonal,* it is allowed *or* permitted.

Licymnia, -ae, *f.,* Licymnia (*mother of Helenor*).

Liger, -grī, *m.,* Liger (*a Trojan*).

lignum, -ī, *n.,* wood ; shaft (413).

līmen, -inis, *n.,* threshold, door ; gate (648).

līmes, -itis, *m.,* path.

linquō, -ere, līquī (3), leave.

liquēfaciō, -ere, -fēcī, -factum, melt.

liquēns, -ntis, liquid, flowing, clear.

liquor (3) *dep.,* am liquid, flow, stream.

lītus, -oris, *n.,* shore, coast.

locus, -ī, *m.,* place : *pl., sometimes neuter,* **loca.,**

longaevus, -a, -um, long-lived, aged ; *as noun,* old-man (650).

longē, *adv.,* from afar ; far off, afar ; *comparat.,* **longius,** further.

longus, -a, -um, long.

loquor, -ī, locūtus (3), *dep.,* speak, say.

lōrīca, -ae, *f.,* corselet, breastplate.

lōrum, -ī, *n.,* rein, trace.

lūceō, -ēre, lūxī (2), gleam, shine.

Lūcetius, -a, -um, Lucetius (*a Rutulian*).

lūctus, -ūs, *m.,* grief, sorrow.

lūcus, -ī, *m.,* grove.

lūdō, -ere, -sī, -sum (3), play, sport.

lūdus, -ī, *m.,* game, play, sport.

lūmen, -inis, *n.,* light.

lūna, -ae, *f.,* moon : *personified* (403).

lupus, -ī, *m.,* wolf.

lūstrō (1), go *or* ride round (58) ; pass through (96).

lūx, lūcis, *f.,* light.

Lycāon, -onis, *m.,* Lycaon.

Lycus, -ī, *m.,* Lycus (*a Trojan*).

Lȳdus, -a, -um, Lydian ; *as noun,* a Lydian.

lympha, -ae, *f.,* water.

Lyncēus, -eī, *m.,* Lynceus (*a Trojan*).

māctus, -a, -um, increased, honoured.

macula, -ae, *f.,* spot.

madeō (2), am wet, moist.

Maeonius, -a, -um, Maeonian, = Lydian, Asiatic.

maestus, -a, -um, sad.
magis, adv., more ; rather.
magister, -trī, m., master ; leader (173, 370).
māgnanimus, -a, -um, great-hearted.
māgnus, -a, -um, great, mighty.
māla, -ae, f., cheek.
male, adv., badly.
mālō, mālle, maluī, prefer.
malum, -ī, n., evil.
mandātum, -ī, n., command.
mandō (1), entrust, command.
mandō, -ere, -dī, -sum (3), (chew), mangle.
maneō, -ēre, mānsī, mānsum (2), remain.
manica, -ae, f., sleeve.
manus, -ūs, f., hand ; band (309), troop : manu, (702), with a blow.
mare, -is, n., sea.
Mārs, Mārtis, m., Mars.
Mārtius, -a, -um, of Mars.
māter, -tris, f., mother.
mātūrus, -a, -um, ripe.
Māvortius, -a, -um, son of Mavors, i.e. Mars.
medium, -ī, n., middle.
medius, -a, -um, middle, in the midst of.
melior, -us, comparat., of bonus, better.
membrum, -ī, n., limb.
meminī, -isse, remember.
memor, -oris, mindful, remembering.
memorō (1), relate, mention.
mēns, mentis, f., mind ; purpose, intent.
meritum, -ī, n., desert, service.

Merops, -opis, m., Merops (a Trojan).
Messāpus, -ī, m., Messapus (leader from Etruria).
metuō, -ere, -uī, -ūtum (3), fear.
metus, -ūs, m., fear.
meus, -a, -um, my, mine.
Mezentius, -ī, m., Mezentius.
micō, -āre, -uī (1), shine.
mīles, -itis, m., soldier.
mīlle, thousand ; mīlia, -ium, n. pl., thousands.
ministrō (1), supply.
minor (1), dep., threaten.
minor, -us, comparat. of parvus, less ; younger (593).
mīrābilis, -e, wonderful, marvellous.
mīror (1), dep., wonder at.
mīrus, -a, -um, wonderful.
misceō, -ēre, -cuī, mixtum (2), mingle.
miser, -era, -erum, wretched, hapless.
miserābilis, -e, pitiable, piteous.
misereor (2), dep., pity, have pity on ; often with gen.
miseret (2), impersonal with acc. and gen., one pities.
mīssilia, -ium, n. pl., missiles, darts, javelins.
mitra, -ae, f., cap.
mittō, -ere, mīsī, mīssum (3), send ; hurl ; fling (663).
Mnestheus, -eī, m., Mnestheus (a Trojan).
modo, adv., only.
modus, -ī, m., manner, way.
moenia, -ium, n. pl., city walls, city.
mōles, -is, f., mass, rampart.

mollis, -e, feeble (341), gentle (817).

moneō (2), advise, warn.

monitus, -ūs, *m.*, warning.

mōns, montis, *m.*, mountain.

mōnstrō (1), point out, show.

mōnstrum, -ī, *n.*, portent.

mora, -ae, *f.*, delay.

morior, -ī, mortuus, *dep.*, die.

moror (1), *dep.*, delay.

mors, mortis, *f.*, death.

mortālis, -e, mortal ; *as noun*, a mortal.

mōs, mōris, *m.*, manner, custom : *in pl.*, *often* = character.

mōtus, -ūs, *m.*, movement.

moveō, -ēre, mōvī, mōtum (2), move ; touch, grieve (471).

mox, *adv.*, soon.

multus, -a, -um, much : *in pl.*, many.

mundus, -ī, *m.*, the universe.

mūrex, -icis, *m.*, purple dye.

mūrus, -ī, *m.*, wall.

mūsa, -ae, *f.*, muse.

mūtō (1), change ; *in pass.*, change (*intrans.*).

mūtus, -a, -um, dumb.

Mycēnae, -ārum, *f. pl.*, Mycenae (*Greek city, capitol of Agamemnon*).

nam, *conj.*, for.

namque, *conj.*, for indeed.

nancīscor, -ī, nactus (3), *dep.*, get, find, light on.

nārrō (1), relate.

nāscor, -ī, nātus (3), *dep.*, am born.

nātus, -ī, *m.*, child, son.

nāvis, -is, *f.*, ship.

-ne, *interrogative enclitic.*

nē, *conj.*, in order that . . . not, lest.

nec, *conj.*, and not, and no, nor : nec non, moreover.

nectō, -ere, -xuī, -xum (3), weave.

nēmō, nēminī, *c.*, no-one, nobody.

nemus, -oris, *n.*, wood.

nepōs, -ōtis, *m.*, grandson, descendant.

Neptūnius, -a, -um, of Neptune.

Neptūnus, -ī, *m.*, Neptune.

neque, *see* nec.

nequeō, -īre, -īvī, am not able, cannot.

nēquīquam, *adv.*, in vain, by no means,

Nērēius, -a, -um, of Nereus (*a god of the sea*).

nervus, -ī, *m.*, bow-string.

neu, neve, *adv.*, and that . . . not.

nī, *conj.*, unless.

niger, -gra, -grum, black.

nigrāns, -ntis, black.

nihil *or* nīl, *indecl. n.*, nothing : *adv.*, in no way.

Nīlus, -ī, *m.*, Nile.

nimbus, -ī, *m.*, storm cloud.

nimis, *adv.*, too much, too.

nimium, *adv.*, too much, too.

nimius, -a, -um, excessive.

Nīsus, -ī, *n.*, Nisus (*a Trojan*).

nitēns, -ntis, shining, bright.

nōdus, -ī, *m.*, knot.

Noēmon, -onis, *m.*, Noemon (*a Trojan*).

nōmen, -inis, *n.*, name.

nōn, *adv.*, not.

nōscō, -ere, nōvī (3), get to know ; *in perfect*, know.

noster, -tra, -trum, our.

nothus, -a, -um, bastard ; *as noun*, a bastard.

nōtus, -a, -um, familiar.

novus, -a, -um, new; strange (110).

nox, noctis, f., night.

nūbes, -is, f., cloud.

nūbilum, -ī, n., cloud.

nūdus, -a, -um, naked.

nūllus, -a, -um, no; none.

Numa, -ae, m., Numa (a Rutulian).

Numānus, -ī, m., Numanus (a Rutulian).

nūmen, -inis, n., divine will or presence; divine protection (247).

numerus, -ī, m., number, note (776).

nunc, adv., now.

nūntius, -ī, m., messenger, message, news (692).

nūper, adv., lately.

nūtō (1), nod.

nutus, -ūs, m., a nod.

O! interj., O! Oh!

obiciō, -ere, -iēcī, -iectum, set in the way, barricade (45); oppose; se obicere, take up positions (379).

oblīvīscor, -ī, oblītus (3), dep., forget; with gen., am forgetful of.

obnītor, -ī, -nīsus, or -nīxus (3), dep. strive or struggle against.

obruō, -ere, -uī, -utum (3), overwhelm.

obscūrus, -a, -um, obscure, dim, dark.

observō (1), observe, note.

obsidiō, -ōnis, f., siege, blockade.

obsīdō (3), beset, invest, blockade.

obstupēscō, -ere, -puī (3), am astounded or struck-dumb.

obtestor (1), dep., appeal to, adjure.

obversus, -a, -um, facing.

obvius, -a, -um, in the way, to meet.

occāsus, -ūs, m., setting.

occulō, -ere, -culuī, -cultum (3), hide.

occultus, -a, -um, hidden.

occupō (1), anticipate.

ōcius, adv., swiftly.

oculus, -ī, m., eye.

offulgeō, -ēre, -sī (2), shine or flash upon.

ōlim, adv., once, formerly; hereafter (99).

olle = ille.

Olympus, -ī, m., Olympus (mountain in N. Greece, home of the gods).

omen, -inis, n., omen.

omnīno, adv., altogether.

omnipotēns, -ntis, almighty.

omnis, -e, all, every.

onerō (1), load, burden.

onerōsus, -a, -um, heavy, weighty.

Opheltes, -ae, m., Opheltes (father of Euryalus).

oppetō, -ere, -petiī, -petītum (3), meet (death); fall (654).

oppidum, -ī, n., town.

oppōnō, -ere, -posuī, -positum (3), put or set in the way of.

opportūnus, -a, -um, convenient.

opprimō, -ere, -pressī, -pressum (3), overwhelm.

(ops), opis, f., help, aid; in pl., means, wealth, resources.

optimus, -a, -um, best (superlat. of bonus).

optō (1), choose, wish, pray.

opus, -eris, n., work.

opus, *indecl.*, need.
ōra, -ae, *f.*, edge.
Orcus, -ī, *m.*, Orcus (*the Under-world*).
ōrdior, -īrī, ōrsus (4) *dep.*, begin.
orior, -īrī, ortus (4), *dep.*, arise ; am born.
ōrō (1), pray for, beg.
Ortygius, -ī, *m.*, Ortygius (*a Rutulian*).
ōs, ōris, *n.*, mouth, face, lips.
os, ossis, *n.*, bone ; *in pl.*, frame (66, 475).
ovīle, -is, *n.*, sheep fold.
ovō (1), rejoice, triumph.

Padus, -ī, *m.*, *the river* Po.
palam, *adv.*, openly.
Palatīnus, -a, -um, of the Pala-tine.
Palīcus, -ī, *m.*, Palicus (*a Sicilian deity*).
Palladium, -ī, *n.*, the Palladium.
Pallantēus, -a, -um, of Pallan-teum.
palma, -ae, *f.*, palm (*of the hand*).
pālor (1) *dep.*, wander ; am dis-persed (780).
Pandarus, -ī, *m.*, Pandarus (*a Trojan*).
papāver, -eris, *n.*, poppy.
par, paris, well-matched, equal.
Parcae, -ārum, *f. pl.*, the Fates.
parcō, -ere, pepercī, parsum (3), spare.
parēns, -ntis, father *or* mother ; forbear (3).
pariter, *adv.*, equally, evenly ; side by side.
parma, -ae, *f.*, shield.
parō (1), make ready, prepare.
pars, partis, *f.*, part.

partus, -ūs, *m.*, bringing forth, birth.
parvus, -a, -um, little, small.
passim, *adv.*, in all directions ; at random.
pateō (2), am *or* lie open.
pater, -tris, *m.*, father ; *in pl.*, leaders (192).
patior, -ī, passus, *dep.*, suffer, allow.
patria, -ae, *f.*, native land.
patrius, -a, -um, of one's father, ancestral.
paulātim, *adv.*, little by little.
pavidus, -a, -um, timid, ner-vous.
pāx, pācis, *f.*, peace.
peccō (1), sin.
pectus, -oris, *n.*, breast, heart.
pecus, -oris, *n.*, cattle.
pelagus, -ī, *m.*, open sea, main.
Pelasgus, -a, -um, Pelasgian = Greek.
pellis, -is, *f.*, skin, hide.
pellō, -ere, pepulī, pulsum (3), drive away, repel.
penātēs, -ium, *m. pl.*, the penates (*household gods*).
pendeō, -ēre, pependī (2), hang ; droop (331).
pendō, -ere, pependī, pēnsum (3), weigh.
penetrālis, -e, inmost ; *in pl. neut. as noun*, chapel, shrine.
penetrō (1) enter, penetrate.
penitus, *adv.*, deeply.
pennātus, -a, -um, winged.
pēnsum, -ī, *n.*, work, office.
per, *prep. with acc.*, through, over, along ; by (104, 105, 258).
peragō, -ere, -ēgī, -āctum (3), finish, accomplish.

percipiō, -ere, -cēpī, -ceptum, perceive, catch, learn (190).

percutiō, -ere, -cussī, -cussum, smite.

perennis, -e, lasting, unceasing.

pereō, -īre, -iī, -itum, perish.

perferō, -ferre, -tulī, -lātum, endure ; bring (news).

perficiō, -ere, -fēcī, -fectum, finish.

perfurō (3), rage furiously.

pergō, -ere, perrēxī, perrēctum (3), proceed, go on.

perīculum or perīclum, -ī, n., danger, peril.

perimō, -ere, -ēmī, -ēmptum (3), destroy.

permittō, -ere, -mīsī, -missum (3), entrust, allow.

permūtō (1), give in exchange.

perōsus, -a, -um, hating, detesting.

perpetior, -ī, -pessus, dep., endure.

perplexus, -a, -um, entangled, intricate.

perrumpō, -ere, -rūpī, -ruptum (3), burst through.

persequor, -ī, -secūtus (3), dep., follow, pursue.

persolvō, -ere, -solvī, -solūtum (3), pay (in full).

perveniō, -īre, -vēnī, -ventum (4), arrive, reach.

pēs, pedis, m., foot ; claw (564).

pestis, -is, f., plague, bane, mischief, danger.

petō, -ere, -īvī, -ītum (3), make for, attack ; seek.

phalārica, -ae, f., the phalarica (a missile).

phalerae, -ārum, f. pl., trappings.

Phaleris, -is, m., Phaleris (a Trojan).

pharetra, -ae, f., quiver.

Phēgēus, -eī, m., Phegeus (a Trojan).

Phoebus, -ī, m., Apollo (as the god of light).

Phrygius, -a, -um, Phrygian ; often = Trojan.

Phryx, -gis, Phrygian ; in pl., = the Trojans.

picea, -ae, f., pitch or forest pine.

piceus, -a, -um, patchy, murky.

pīctus, -a, -um, embroidered.

pietās, -ātis, f., dutiful behaviour.

pīla, -ae, f., pier, mole.

Pīlumnus, -ī, m., Pilumnus (ancestor of Turnus).

pīneus, -a, -um, of fir.

pingō, -ere, pīnxī, pīctum (3), paint, embroider.

pinguis, -e, rich, fertile.

pīnus, -ūs, f., pine, pine-torch.

pius, -a, -um, good.

pix, picis, f., pitch.

plācābilis, -ē, readily appeased.

placidus, -a, -um, calm, peaceful.

plaga, -ae, f., district, quarter.

plēbs, plēbis, f., multitude (343), folk.

plēnus, -a, -um, full.

plumbum, -ī, n., lead.

plūrimus, -a, -um, most, very much.

pluvia, -ae, f., rain.

pluviālis, -e, rainy.

pōculum, -ī, n., cup.

poena, -ae, f., recompense, retribution ; penalty.

polliceor (2), dep., promise.

polus, -ī, m., sky.

pondus, -eris, n., weight.

pōnō, -ere, posuī, positum (3), put or place ; lay aside.

pōns, pontis, *m.*, bridge.

pontus, -ī, *m.*, sea.

poples, -itis, *m.*, ham, hollow (*of the knee*).

populus, -ī, *m.*, people.

porrigō, -ere, -rēxī, -rēctum (3), stretch out ; porrectus (589), at full length.

porrō, *adv.*, furthermore.

porta, -ae, *f.*, door, gate.

portō (1), carry, bring.

portus, -ūs, *m.*, harbour.

poscō, -ere, poposcī (3), demand ; require ; pray for.

possum, posse, potuī, am able, can.

post, *adv.*, *and prep. with acc.*, afterwards ; after, behind.

postis, -is, *m.*, door post.

postrēmus, -a, -um, last.

potestās, -ātis, *f.*, power.

potior (4), *dep.*, gain possession of; *often with abl.*

potis, -e, able.

prae, *adv.*, *and prep. with abl.*, in front of.

praebeō (2), offer, provide.

praecēdō, -ere, -cessī, -cessum (3), go before, precede.

praeceps, -cipitis, headlong, with headlong haste.

praeceptum, -ī, *n.*, instruction.

praecipiō, -ere, -cēpī, -ceptum, instruct, order.

praecipitō (1), rush ; hurl themselves upon (670).

praecordia, -ōrum, *n. pl.*, (midriff), breast, heart (413).

praeda, -ae, *f.*, spoil, booty.

praefīgō, -ere, -xī, -xum (3), fix in front *or* on.

praemittō, -ere, -mīsī, -mīssum (3), send before *or* on ahead.

praemium, -ī, *n.*, prize, reward.

praeripiō, -ere, -ripuī, -reptum, seize before *or* first ; steal.

praesēns, -ntis, present.

praesentia, -ae, *f.*, presence.

praetendō, -ere, -dī, -tum (3), set in front.

praetereā, *adv.*, besides, moreover; in addition.

precor (1), *dep.*, pray.

prehendō (prendō), -ere, -dī, -sum (3), take, seize.

premō, -ere, -ssī, -ssum (3), press ; check (324).

pretium, -ī, *n.*, price.

(prex, precis) *f.*, *only in plural, with acc. dat. and abl.*, *sg.*, prayer, entreaty.

Priamus, -ī, *m.*, Priam (*king of Troy*).

prīmaevus, -a, -um, youthful ; in the first bloom of life (545).

prīmō, *adv.*, at first.

prīmum, *adv.*, first.

prīmus, -a, -um, first, foremost (479) ; *as noun*, chieftain, leader.

prīnceps, -cipis, first, foremost ; *as noun*, chieftain, captain.

principium, -ī, *n.*, beginning.

prior, -us, ahead, former, first.

prīscus, -a, -um, ancient.

prius, *adv.*, sooner, before.

Privernus, -ī, *m.*, Privernus (*a Rutulian*).

prō, *prep. with abl.*, on behalf of, for ; in front of.

prōcēdō, -ere, -cessī (3), advance.

procerēs, -um, *m. pl.*, chieftains, princes, nobles.

Prochyta, -ae, *f.*, Prochyta (*an island*).

procul, *adv.*, afar off, from afar.

prōcumbō, -ere, -cubuī, -cubitum (3), lie prostrate (190).

prōcūrō (1), attend to, refresh.

prōcurrō, -ere, -currī, -cursum (3) run forward.

prōdō, -ere, -didī, -ditum (3), betray.

prōdūcō, -ere, -xī, -ctum (3), lead forth.

proelium, -ī, *n.*, battle.

prōflō (1), breathe heavily.

prohibeō (2), hold back, check.

prōiciō, -ere, -iēcī, -iectum, cast forth *or* down.

prōlēs, -is, *f.*, offspring ; race.

promittō, -ere, -mīsī, -missum (3), promise.

Promolus, -ī, *m.*, Promolus (*a Trojan*).

prōnus, -a, -um, forwards, falling *or* with head forward.

properē, *adv.*, hurriedly, hastily.

properō (1), hasten, hurry.

properus, -a, -um, quick, speedy.

propinquō (1), draw near.

propior, -us, nearer.

propter, *prep. with acc.*, on account of ; near by (680).

prōpūgnāculum, -ī, *n.*, bulwark, tower.

prōra, -ae, *f.*, prow.

prōsequor, -ī, -secūtus (3), *dep.*, follow, attend, escort (310).

prōspectō (1), look forth, behold, see.

prōspiciō, -ere, -spēxi, -spectum, look out, descry.

prōsum, -esse, -fuī, am of advantage (to) ; avail.

prōtinus, *adv.*, forthwith.

prōturbō (1), assail, repel.

proximus, -a, -um, nearest, next.

Prytanis, -is, *m.*, Prytanis (*a Trojan*).

pūbēs, -is, *f.*, youth ; young men.

pudet (2), *impersonal*, it shames.

pudor, -ōris, *m.*, shame.

puer, -erī, *m.*, boy.

pūgna, -ae, *f.*, fight, combat.

pulcher, -chra, -chrum, beauteous, fine, fair, lovely.

pūlmō, -ōnis, *m.*, lung.

pulsō (1), beat, strike, shake (415).

pulvis, -eris, *m.*, dust.

puppis, -is, *f.*, stern, ship.

purpureus, -a, -um, crimson ; bright (435).

quā, *adv.*, where? in any way ; anywhere.

quaerō, -ere, -sīvī, -sītum (3), seek, ask.

quālis, -e (such) as, like.

quam, *adv.*, than ; as.

quandō, *adv., and conj.*, ever ; when, since.

quantus, -a, -um, *interrog.*, how great ; *relative*, as.

quassō (1), shake ; brandish (521).

quatiō, -ere, —, quassum, shake.

-que, and ; -que . . . que, both . . . and.

Quercēns, -ntis, *m.*, Quercens (*a Rutulian*).

quercus, -ūs, *f.*, oak.

questus, -ūs, *m.*, complaint.

quī, qua, quid, *indefinite adj.*, any.

quī, quae, quod, *relat. pronoun*, who, which, that ; what.

quīcunque, quae-, quod-, whoever, whatever.

quid, *adv.*, why?

quidem, *adv.*, indeed.

quiēs, -ētis, *f.*, rest.
quiēscō, -ere, -ēvī, -ētum (3), keep quiet, rest.
quīn, *conj.*, why not?
quis, quid, *indefin. pronoun*, anyone, anything.
quis, quid, *interrog. pronoun*, who? which? what?
quisque, quae-, quid- (*adj.* quod-), *indefin. pronoun*, each.
quisquis, quisquid, *rel. pronoun*, whoever, whatever.
quō, *adv.*, whither ; to which.
quod, *conj.*, because.
quondam, *adv.*, once, of yore ; at times.
quoniam, *conj.*, since.
quoque, *adv.*, also.
quot, *indeclin.*, how many? (as many) as.

rabiēs, -ēī, *f.*, rage, fury.
radius, -ī, *m.*, ray ; shuttle.
rāmus, -ī, *m.*, branch, bough.
rapiō, -ere, -uī, raptum, seize, snatch ; hurry (211) ; rescue (213) ; plunder (613).
rārus, -a, -um, sparse, thin.
rāstrum, -ī, *n.*, mattock.
ratiō, -ōnis, *f.*, method, plan.
ratis, -is, *f.*, (raft) ; ship, bark.
ratus, -a, -um, ratified, valid.
raucus, -a, -um, hoarse.
recēns, -ntis, fresh.
recipiō, -ere, -cēpī, -ceptum, recover ; welcome (727).
reclūdō, -ere, -clūsī, -clūsum (3), open ; draw, unsheathe (423).
rector, -ōris, *m.*, director, leader ; ruler (173).
recumbō, -ere, -cubuī (3), lie *or* sink down.

reddō, -ere, -didī, -ditum (3), give back.
redeō, -īre, -īvī (-iī), -itum, return.
redimīculum, -ī, *n.*, string.
redimō, -ere, -ēmī, -ēmptum (3), ransom.
redūcō, -ere, -xī, -ctum (3), lead *or* bring back.
redux, -ducis, returning, returned.
referō, -ferre, rettulī, relātum, carry, bring, *or* bear back ; disgorge (350) ; retrace (798).
refluō (3), flow back.
refulgeō, -ēre, -sī (2), flash back, reflect.
rēgia, -ae, *f.*, palace.
regiō, -ōnis, *f.*, direction ; region.
rēgnum, -ī, *n.*, kingdom, realm.
regō, -ere, -xī, -ctum (3), direct, rule ; guide.
religō (1), fasten, tie up ; tether (352).
relinquō, -ere, -līquī, -lictum (3), leave behind, leave.
remittō, -ere, -mīsī, -missum (3), send back.
remūgiō (4), re-echo, resound.
Remulus, -ī, *m.*, Remulus (*surname of Numanus*).
Remus, -ī, *m.*, Remus (*a Rutulian*).
reor, rērī, ratus (2), *dep.*, think.
repente, *adv.*, suddenly.
reperiō, -īre, repperī, repertum (4), discover.
repōnō, -ere, -posuī, -positum (3), put back, replace.
reportō (1), bring *or* carry back.
requiēs, -ētis, *f.*, rest, repose.
requīrō, -ere, -quīsīvī, -quīsītum (3), seek.
rēs, reī, *f.*, thing ; *in pl.*, fortune.

rescindō, -ere, -scidī, -scissum (3), cut, tear open.

resīdō, -ere, -sēdī (3), settle ; draw (back) (539).

resolvō, -ere, -vī, -solūtum (3) loosen.

respiciō, -ere, -spēxī, -spectum, look back at.

respīrō (1), regain or recover breath.

respondeō, -ēre, -dī, -nsum (2), reply.

respōnsum, -ī, n., reply, answer.

retegō, -ere, -tēxī, -tēctum (3), reveal.

retrō, adv., backwards.

revellō, -ere, -vellī, -vulsum (3), tear off.

revocō (1), call back, recall.

revolvō, -ere, -vī, -volūtum (3), roll back

rēx, rēgis, m., king, prince.

Rhamnēs, -ētis, m., Rhamnes (a Rutulian augur).

Rhoetus, -ī, m., Rhoetus (a Rutulian).

rigō (1), water, bedew.

rīpa, -ae, f., bank.

rīte, adv., duly, aright.

rīvus, -ī, m., stream.

Rōmānus, -a, -um, Roman.

roseus, -a, -um, rosy.

rōstrum, -ī, n., beak, prow (of ship).

rota, -ae, f., wheel.

rotō (1), wheel, whirl (441).

rubēns, -ntis, red.

rubeō (2), am red.

ruber, -bra, -brum, red.

rudis, -e, rough, rudely finished (743).

ruīna, -ae, f., falling, crash.

rūmor, -ōris, m., rumour.

rumpō, -ere, rūpī, ruptum (3), break, burst ; lay bare (432) ; cleave (580).

ruō, -ere, -uī, -ūtum (3), rush, hurry : speed (474).

rūrsus, adv., again.

Rutulus, -ī, m., a Rutulian.

sacer, -cra, -crum, holy, sacred.

sacrō (1), consecrate.

sacrum, -ī, n., sacrifice ; in pl. sacred rites, offerings.

saepiō, -īre, -psī, -ptum (4), fence ; compass (783).

saeviō (4), rage, storm.

saevus -a, -um, cruel, fierce.

Sagaris, -is, m., Sagaris (a Trojan).

sagitta, -ae, f., arrow.

saltus, -ūs, m., leap.

salūs, -ūtis, f., safety.

sanguīneus, -a, -um, blood-red.

sanguis, -inis, m., blood.

Sarpēdōn, -onis, m., Sarpedon (king of Lycia).

sat or satis, adv., enough.

Sāturnius, -a, -um, sprung from Saturn.

saxeus, -a, -um, of stone.

saxum, -ī, n., stone, rock.

scālae, -ārum, f. pl., ladder.

scelerātus, -a, -um, villainous wicked.

scēptrum, -ī, n., sceptre.

scindō, -ere, scidī, scissum (3), tear down.

scūtātus, -a, -um, armed with a shield.

scūtum, -ī, n., shield.

sē or sēsē, gen. suī, reflexive pronoun, 3rd pers., himself, herself, itself ; themselves.

secō, -āre, -uī, sectum (1), cut.
cleave.

secundus, -a, -um, following (of winds) ; second, favourable.

sed, conj., but.

sēdātus, -a, -um, peaceful.

sedeō, -ēre, sēdī, sessum (2), sit, sit down.

sēdēs, -is, f., seat, abode.

sēgnis, -e, slow, inactive, cowardly.

semel, adv., once.

(sēminēx), -necis, half-dead.

sēmita, -ae, f., path.

semper, adv., always.

senecta, -ae, f., old age.

senectūs, -ūtis, f., old age.

senex, senis, m., old man.

sententia, -ae, f., thought, opinion.

sentēs, -ium, m. pl., thorns, briars.

sentiō, -īre, sēnsī, sēnsum (4), feel, perceive.

septem, seven.

sepulcrum, -ī, n., grave, tomb.

sequor, -ī, secūtus (3), dep., follow, follow up (636).

serēnus, -a, -um, bright, clear, calm.

Serestus, -ī, m., Serestus (a Trojan).

sermō, -ōnis, m., talking, conversation ; words.

Serrānus, -ī, m., Serranus (a Rutulian).

sērus, -a, -um, late.

serva, -ae, f., female slave.

servō (1), save, keep ; take (222).

sēsē, see sē.

sētius, comparat. adverb, otherwise ; less.

seu, see sīve.

sex, six.

sī, conj., if.

sīc, adv., in this way, thus.

siccus, -a, -um, dry, parched.

Sīdōnius, -a, -um, Sidonian, Phoenician.

sīdus, -eris, n., star, constellation.

sīgnō (1), mark.

sīgnum, -ī, n., mark, sign ; figure (263) ; watchword (394).

silēns, -ntis, silent.

sileō (2), am silent.

silva, -ae, f., wood, forest.

silvester, -tris, -tre, of a forest.

similis, -e, like.

simul, adj., at the same time ; simul atque (ac), as soon as.

sine, prep. with abl., without.

singultō (1), sob.

singultus, -ūs, m., sobbing, gasping.

sinister, -tra, -trum, on the left, left.

sinō, -ere, sīvī, situm (3), let, allow.

sīve or seu, conj., or if ; whether, or.

sociō (1), unite.

socius, -ī, m., comrade, companion.

sōl, sōlis, m., sun.

soleō, -ēre, solitus (2), semi-dep., am wont or accustomed ; perf. part., solitus, accustomed.

solidus, -a, -um, solid.

sollemnis, -e, annual, yearly (626), customary.

sollicitus, -a, -um, anxious.

sōlor (1), dep., console, comfort.

solum, -ī, n., soil, ground.

sōlus, -a, -um, alone.

solvō, -ere, -vī, solūtum (3), loose, relax (189).

somnus, -ī, *m.*, sleep.
sonitus, -ūs, *m.*, sound.
sonō, -āre, -uī, -itum (1), sound, ring.
sonor, -ōris, *m.*, noise, sound.
sonus, -ī, *m.*, sound.
sors, sortis, *f.*, lot, allotment.
sortior (4), *dep.*, allot.
spargō, -ere, -sī, -sum (3), sprinkle.
spatium -ī, *n.*, space ; interval.
spectō (1), look at.
specus, -ūs, *m.*, cave.
spērō (1), hope.
spēs, -eī, *f.*, hope.
spīculum, -ī, *n.*, dart.
spīrāmentum, -ī, *n.*, breathing-hole.
spīrō (1), breathe.
spissus, -a, -um, thick.
spolium, -ī, *n.*, spoil.
spondeō, -ēre, spopondī, spōnsum (2), pledge, promise.
spūmō (1), foam.
squāma, -ae, *f.*, scale.
stabulum, -ī, *n.*, stall.
statiō, -ōnis, *f.*, post, sentry duty (183).
statuō, -ere, -uī, -ūtum (3), place, set.
stella, -ae, *f.*, star.
sternō, -ere, strāvī, strātum (3), lay low ; strew (666).
stimulus, -ī, *m.*, goad, spur.
stirps, stirpis, *f.*, stock, family, lineage.
stō, -āre, stetī, statum (1), stand.
stomachus, -ī, *m.*, gullet.
strāgēs, -is, *f.*, overthrow, destruction.
strepitus, -ūs, *m.*, din.

strepō, -ere, -uī (3), rattle, hum, roar ; ring (808).
strīdō (3), whizz ; whirr (419).
stringō, -ere, -nxī, -ctum (3), graze ; flash on (294).
struō, -ere, -xī, -ctum (3), build.
Stygius, -a, -um, Stygian.
suādeō, -ēre, -sī, -sum (3), urge ; urge on.
sub, *prep. with acc.*, under, up towards ; *with abl.*, under, beneath.
subeō, -īre, -īvī, (-iī), -itum, approach.
subitō, *adv.*, suddenly.
subitus, -a, -um, sudden.
sublīmis, -e, aloft, on high.
sublūstris, -e, dim, glimmering.
subrīdeō, -ēre, -sī, -sum (2), smile.
subsistō, -ere, -stitī (3), withstand, hold my own.
subter, *prep. with acc. and abl.*, under, below, beneath.
succēdō, -ere, -cessī, -cessum (3), take place of ; enter into again (663).
succīdō, -ere, -cīdī, -cīsum (3), cut down.
succurrō, -ere, -currī, -cursum (3), help, aid, (*often with dat.*).
sūdor, -ōris, *m.*, sweat.
sufficiō, -ere, -fēcī, -fectum, supply ; grant (803) ; avail for (810).
Sulmō, -ōnis, *m.*, Sulmo (*a Latin*).
sum, esse, fuī, am.
summus, -a, -um, highest, loftiest, top.
sūmō, -ere, sūmpsī, sūmptum (3), take.
super, *adv.*, above.
super, *prep. with acc.*, over, on ; *with abl.*, above, at.

superbus, -a, -um, proud, haughty.

superō (1), overcome ; pass (314).

supersum, -esse, -fuī, survive, remain, am left.

superus, -a, -um, upper ; *in masc. pl.,* the gods above.

supīnus, -a, -um, upturned.

supplex, -icis, suppliant.

suprā, *prep. with acc.,* above.

surgō, -ere, surrēxī (3), rise.

suscipiō, -ere, -cēpī, -ceptum, undertake.

suscitō, (1), arouse.

suspectus, -ūs, *m.* (looking up), height.

suspendō, -ere, -dī, -nsum (3), hang up.

suspiciō, -ere, -spēxī, -spectum, look up.

sustineō, -ēre, -tinuī, -tentum (2), support, withstand.

suus, -a, -um, his, her, its, their own.

Sȳmaethius, -a, -um, of Symaethus (*a river in Sicily*).

tabula, -ae, *f.,* plank.

tābum, -ī, *n.,* gore.

tacitus, -a, -um, silent.

taeda, -ae, *f.,* pine-torch.

Tagus, -ī, *m.,* Tagus (*a Latin*).

talentum, -ī, *n.,* a talent.

tālis, -e, such.

tam, *adv.,* so.

tamen, *adv.,* nevertheless ; after all.

tandem, *adv.,* at length ; at last.

tangō, -ere, tetigī, tāctum (3), touch ; reach (135), move deeply (138).

tantum, *adv.,* so much, only.

tantus, -a, -um, so big *or* great ; such great.

tapēs, -ētis, *m.,* rug.

tardus, -a, -um, slow, sluggish.

Tartara, -ōrum, *n. pl.,* the lower world.

taureus, -a, -um, of a bull.

tēctum, -ī, *n.,* roof : home, house.

tēgmen, -inis, *n.,* covering.

tegō, -ere, -xī, -ctum (3), cover ; protect (50) ; conceal ; shroud (488).

tēla, -ae, *f.,* web.

tellūs, -ūris, *f.,* earth, land.

tēlum, -ī, *n.,* missile, weapon.

temerē, *adv.,* carelessly, heedlessly.

tempestās, -ātis, *f.,* weather ; storm.

templum, -ī, *n.,* temple.

temptō (1), make trial of ; try, attempt.

tempus, -oris, *n.,* time, season ; temple (*of head*).

tendō, -ere, tetendī, tentum *or* **tēnsum** (3), stretch ; aim, strive, make one's way (351, 555).

tenebrae, -arum, *f. pl.,* darkness.

teneō, -ēre, -uī (2), hold, keep ; man (470) ; gain.

tener, -era, -erum, tender ; yielding (699).

tenuis, -e, thin, fine.

tepefaciō, -ere, -fēcī, -factum, make warm.

tepēscō (3), grow warm.

tepidus, -a, -um, warm.

ter, *adv.,* thrice.

tergum, -ī, *n.,* back, hide ; **a tergo,** from behind ; **terga dare** (686), to flee.

terō, -ere, trīvī, trītum (3), (rub), wear; spend (*of time*).

terra, -ae, *f.,* earth, land.

terreō (2), frighten, scare.

terribilis, -e, terrifying.

terror, -ōris, *m.,* panic, terror.

testis, -is, *c.,* witness.

testor (1), *dep.,* call to witness.

testūdō, -inis, *f.* (tortoise); roof of shields.

Teucrī, -ōrum, *m. pl.,* the Teucri, i.e. the Trojans.

thalamus, -ī, *m.,* marriage.

Thaumantias, -iadis, *f.,* daughter of Thaumas.

Thēbānus, -a, -um, Theban, of Thebe.

Themilla, -ae, *m.,* Themilla (*a Rutulian*).

tholus, -ī, *m.,* dome.

Thrācius, -a, -um, Thracian.

Tiberīnus, -ī, *m., the river* Tiber.

tibia, -ae, *f.,* pipe, flute.

Tīburs, -tis, of Tibur.

tigris, -is, *f.,* tigress.

timeō (2), fear.

timor, -ōris, *m.,* fear; *personified* (719).

tinnītus, -ūs, *m.,* rattling.

Tithōnus, -ī, *m.,* Tithonus.

Tmarus, -ī, *m.,* Tmarus (*a Rutulian*).

tollō, -ere, sustulī, sublātum (3), lift, raise; bear, rear.

tonō, -āre, -uī (1), thunder.

torpeō (2), am numbed (499) *or* palsied.

torqueō, -ēre, -sī, -tum (2), turn (724); hurl; direct, guide (93); poise (402); whirl (671).

torrēns, -ntis, seething, in turmoil.

torus, -ī, *m.,* couch.

tot, *indecl.,* so many.

totidem, *indecl.,* just so many.

tōtus, -a, -um, whole.

trabs, -is, *f.,* beam, tree.

trahō, -ere, -xī, -ctum (3), draw, drag.

trāiciō, -ere, -iēcī, -iectum, pierce, cleave.

trānsabeō, -īre, -iī, pierce, transfix.

trānscurrō, -ere, -currī, -cursum (3), run *or* shoot across.

transeō, -īre, -iī, -itum, go through, pierce, pass through (413).

trānsfodiō, -ere, -fōdī, -fossum, pierce, transfix.

trānsigō, -ere, -ēgī, -āctum (3), drive through, pierce.

tremefaciō, -ere, -fēcī, -factum, make to tremble.

tremō, -ere, -uī, (3), tremble.

trepidō (1), am alarmed *or* anxious *or* confused.

trepidus, -a, -um, alarmed, nervous; impatient.

trēs, tria, three.

tripūs, -podis, *m.,* tripod.

trīstis, -e, sad, gloomy.

Trōia, -ae, *f.,* Troy.

Trōiānus, -a, -um, Trojan; *as noun,* a Trojan.

Trōs, -ōis, Trojan.

truncus, -ī, *m.,* stem, trunk.

tū, tuī, thou.

tuba, -ae, *f.,* trumpet.

tueor (2), *dep.,* look at, gaze upon, guard (175); glare (794).

tum, *adv.,* then.

tumidus, -a, -um., swelling.

tumultus, -ūs, *m.,* uproar, tumult; onset (397).

tumulus, -ī, *m.,* hill; mound.

tunica, -ae, f., tunic.
turba, -ae, f., crowd, throng.
turbidus, -a, -um, wild, confused, violent.
turbō (1), throw into confusion; bewilder; make havoc (339).
turbō, -inis, m., hurricane, whirlwind.
Turnus, -ī, m., Turnus (leader of the Rutulians).
turris, -is, f., tower.
tūtus, -a, -um, safe.
tuus, -a, -um, thy.
tympanum, -ī, n., drum, timbrel.
Typhōeūs, -eī, m., Typhoeus.
Tyrrhīdae, -ārum, m. pl., sons of Tyrrhus.

ubi, adv., where, when.
ūllus, -a, -um, any.
ultimus, -a, -um, last.
ultrā, adv., beyond, further.
ultrō, adv., of one's own accord, voluntarily; unasked; actually.
ululātus, -ūs, m., wailing.
umbō, -ōnis, m., boss (of shield).
umbra, -ae, f., shade.
umerus, -ī, m., shoulder.
umquam, adv., ever.
ūnā, adv., together; at the same moment (631).
uncus, -a, -um, hooked.
unda, -ae, f., wave, water: flood (700).
unde, adv., whence, from which.
undique, adv., from or on all sides.
ungō, -ere, -nxī, -nctum (3), smear.
ūnus, -a, -um, one: alone, only.
urbs, urbis, f., city.
urgeō, -ēre, ursī (2), encourage (73); work hard at (489).

ūrō, -ere, ussī, ūstum (3), burn.
usquam, adv., anywhere.
ut, conj., when, as; in order that, that.
uterque, utraque, utrumque, each (of two); both.
ūtor, -ī, ūsus (3), dep., use (with abl.).

vadum -ī, n., shoal, ford.
vāgīna, -ae, f., sheath.
valeō (2), am strong; am able, have power.
vallis, -is, f., valley.
vāllum, -ī, n., rampart.
variō (1), vary.
varius, -a, -um, varied, different.
vāstātor, -ōris, m., destroyer.
vāstus, -a, -um, vast, immense, huge.
-ve, or.
vehō, -ere, vēxī, vēctum (3), carry, bear.
vel, conj., or.
vellō, -ere, vulsī, vulsum (3), pluck, tear down.
velut (velutī), adv., even as.
venābulum, -ī, n., hunting-spear.
vēnātrīx, -īcis, f., huntress.
vēnātus, -ūs, m., hunting.
venēnum, -ī, n., poison.
veneror (1), dep., worship; venerandus, revered, august.
venio, -īre, vēnī, ventum (4) come.
vēnor (1), dep., hunt.
ventus, -ī, m., wind.
Venus, -eris, f., Venus.
verberō (1), lash.
verbum, -ī, n., word.
vērē, adv., truly.
vereor (2), dep., fear.
vērō, adv., in truth, in fact.

versō (1), turn ; brandish (747).
vertex, -icis, *m.*, top, head.
vertō, -ere, -tī, -sum (3), turn ; ply (718).
vērus, -a, -um, true.
vēsānus, -a, -um, mad.
Vesta, -ae, *f.*, Vesta.
vester, -tra, -trum, your.
vestīgium, -ī, *n.*, footstep.
vestis, -is, *f.*, garment, robe.
vetō, -āre, -uī, -itum (1), forbid.
vetus, -eris, old, ancient.
vetustus, -a, -um, old, ancient.
via, -ae, *f.*, road, path.
vibrō (1), brandish, poise.
vicis, *gen. of a nom. sg. not found,* with acc. **vicem**, abl. **vice** ; *pl.* **vices**, **vices**, **vicibus**, turn.
vīctor, -ōris, *m.*, victor, conqueror; *as adj.*, victorious.
videō, -ēre, -dī, -sum (2), see : *in pass.*, seem, appear.
vigil, -ilis, watchful ; *as noun,* watchman.
vigilō (1), watch.
vīgintī, twenty.
vigor, -ōris, *m.*, force, vigour.
vincō, -ere, vīcī, vīctum (3), conquer, overcome.
vinculum, -ī, *n.*, chain ; cable (118).
vīnum, -ī, *n.*, wine.
vir, virī, *m.*, man, hero, warrior.

virgineus, -a, -um, of a maiden.
virgō, -inis, *f.*, virgin, maiden.
virīlis, -e, of a man, manly.
virtus, -ūtis, *f.*, worth, valour (634); prowess.
vīs, *acc.*, **vim**, *abl.*, **vī**, *f.*, force, violence ; *pl.* **vīrēs**, -ium, strength, might, power.
vīta, -ae, *f.*, life.
vīvō, -ere, vīxī (3), live.
vix, *adv.*, scarcely.
vōciferor (1), *dep.*, shout, bawl.
vocō (1), call ; summon (320).
Volcānus, -ī, *m.*, Vulcan (*god of fire*) ; fire.
Volcēns, -ntis, Volcens (*a Latin*).
volitō (1), flit, flutter.
volō (1), fly.
volō, **velle**, **voluī**, wish, will, am willing.
Volscī, -ōrum, *m. pl.*, the Volsci.
volvō, -ere, -vī, -ūtum (3), roll : *pass.* = *English intran.*, roll (36, 414).
vomō, -ere, -uī, -itum (3), vomit, pour *or* belch forth.
vorāgō, -inis, *f.*, whirlpool, eddy.
vōs, *pl. of* **tū**, you.
vōtum, -ī, *n.*, vow, prayer.
vōx, vōcis, *f.*, voice, word ; sound.
vulnus, -eris, *n.*, wound.
vultus, -ūs, *m.*, face, countenance ; features.

BRISTOL CLASSICAL PRESS

LATIN LIST

ADVANCED LATIN UNSEENS
Drawn from the selection of COOK and MARCHANT by ANTHONY BOWEN

AMMIANUS MARCELLINUS; A Selection
Text with Introduction and Notes by R. C. BLOCKLEY

CICERO: *PHILIPPICS I & II*
Edited by J. D. DENNISTON

CICERO: *PRO MILONE*
Edited with Introduction and Notes by F. H. COLSON

CICERO: *VERRINE V*
Edited with Introduction, Notes and Vocabulary by R. G. C. LEVENS

HORACE IN HIS *ODES*
Selected *Odes* with running Commentary and Vocabularies by J. A. HARRISON

JUVENAL: *SATIRES I, III, X*
Text with Introduction and Notes by N. RUDD and E. COURTNEY

LATIN LOVE ELEGY
Selections with Introduction and Notes by R. MALTBY

LUCAN: *DE BELLO CIVILI VII*
Text with Introduction and Notes by O. A. W. DILKE

OVID: *AMORES I*
Edited with Translation and running Commentary by JOHN BARSBY

OVID: *METAMORPHOSES III*
Text with Introduction, Notes and Vocabulary by A. A. R. HENDERSON

OVID: *METAMORPHOSES XI*
Edited with Introduction, Notes and Vocabulary by G. M. H. MURPHY

RES PUBLICA: Roman Politics and Society according to Cicero
By W. K. LACEY & B. W. J. G. WILSON

ROMAN DECLAMATION
Texts with Introduction and Notes by MICHAEL WINTERBOTTOM

SALLUST: *BELLUM CATILINAE*
Text with Introduction and Notes by PATRICK McGUSHIN

SALLUST: ROME AND JUGURTHA
Text with Introduction and Notes by J. R. HAWTHORN

SENECA THE YOUNGER: Selected Prose
Texts with Introduction and Notes by H. MacL. CURRIE

SILVER LATIN EPIC: An Approach
Texts with Introduction and Notes by H. MacL. CURRIE

SUETONIUS: *DIVUS AUGUSTUS*
Text with Introduction and Notes by J. M. CARTER

SUETONIUS: *NERO*
Text with Introduction and Notes by B. H. WARMINGTON

VIRGIL: *AENEID VIII*
Edited by H. E. GOULD and J. L. WHITELEY

VIRGIL: *AENEID IX*
Edited by J. L. WHITELEY

VIRGIL: *GEORGICS I & IV*
Edited by H. H. HUXLEY

BRISTOL CLASSICAL PRESS

GREEK LIST